Lecture Notes in Economics and Mathematical Systems

For information about Vols. 1–100, please contact your bookseller or Springer-Verlag

Vol. 101: W. M. Wonham, Linear Multivariable Control. A Geometric Approach. X, 344 pages. 1974.

Vol. 102: Analyse Convexe et Ses Applications. Comptes Rendus, Janvier 1974. Edited by J.-P. Aubin. IV, 244 pages. 1974.

Vol. 103: D. E. Boyce, A. Farhi, R. Weischedel, Optimal Subset Selection. Multiple Regression, Interdependence and Optimal Network Algorithms. XIII, 187 pages. 1974.

Vol. 104: S. Fujino, A Neo-Keynesian Theory of Inflation and Economic Growth. V, 96 pages. 1974.

Vol. 105: Optimal Control Theory and its Applications. Part I. Proceedings 1973. Edited by B. J. Kirby. VI, 425 pages. 1974.

Vol. 106: Optimal Control Theory and its Applications. Part II. Proceedings 1973. Edited by B. J. Kirby. VI, 403 pages. 1974.

Vol. 107: Control Theory, Numerical Methods and Computer Systems Modeling. International Symposium, Rocquencourt, June 17–21, 1974. Edited by A. Bensoussan and J. L. Lions. VIII, 757 pages. 1975.

Vol. 108: F. Bauer et al. Supercritical Wing Sections II. A Handbook. V, 296 pages. 1975.

Vol. 109: R. von Randow, Introduction to the Theory of Matroids. IX, 102 pages. 1975.

Vol. 110: C. Striebel, Optimal Control of Discrete Time Stochastic Systems. III, 208 pages. 1975.

Vol. 111: Variable Structure Systems with Application to Economics and Biology. Proceedings 1974. Edited by A. Ruberti and R. R. Mohler. VI, 321 pages. 1975.

Vol. 112: J. Wilhelm, Objectives and Multi-Objective Decision Making Under Uncertantly. IV, 111 pages. 1975.

Vol. 113: G. A. Aschinger, Stabilitätsaussagen über Klassen von Matrizen mit verschwindenden Zeilensummen. V, 102 Seiten 1975.

Vol. 114: G. Uebe, Produktionstheorie. XVII, 301 Seiten. 1976.

Vol. 115: Anderson et al., Foundations of System Theory: Finitary and Infinitary Conditions. VII, 93 pages. 1976

Vol. 116: K. Miyazawa, Input-Output Analysis and the Structure of Income Distribution. IX, 135 pages. 1976.

Vol. 117: Optimization and Operations Research. Proceedings 1975. Edited by W. Oettli and K. Ritter. IV, 316 pages. 1976.

Vol. 118: Traffic Equilibrium Methods, Proceedings 1974. Edited by M. A. Florian. XXIII, 432 pages. 1976.

Vol. 119: Inflation in Small Countries. Proceedings 1974. Edited by H. Frisch. VI, 356 pages. 1976.

Vol. 120: G. Hasenkamp, Specification and Estimation of Multiple-Output Production Functions. VII, 151 pages. 1976.

Vol. 121: J. W. Cohen, On Regenerative Processes in Queueing Theory. IX, 93 pages. 1976.

Vol. 122: M. S. Bazaraa, and C. M. Shetty,Foundations of Optimization VI. 193 pages. 1976

Vol. 123: Multiple Criteria Decision Making. Kyoto 1975. Edited by M. Zeleny. XXVII, 345 pages. 1976.

Vol. 124: M. J. Todd. The Computation of Fixed Points and Applications. VII, 129 pages. 1976.

Vol. 125: Karl C. Mosler. Optimale Transportnetze. Zur Bestimmung ihres kostengünstigsten Standorts bei gegebener Nachfrage. VI, 142 Seiten. 1976.

Vol. 126: Energy, Regional Science and Public Policy. Energy and Environment I. Proceedings 1975. Edited by M. Chatterji and P. Van Rompuy. VIII, 316 pages. 1976.

Vol. 127: Environment, Regional Science and Interregional Modeling. Energy and Environment II. Proceedings 1975. Edited by M. Chatterji and P. Van Rompuy. IX, 211 pages. 1976.

Vol. 128: Integer Programming and Related Areas. A Classified Bibliography. Edited by C. Kastning. XII, 495 pages. 1976.

Vol. 129: H.-J. Lüthi, Komplementaritäts- und Fixpunktalgorithmen in der mathematischen Programmierung. Spieltheorie und Ökonomie. VII, 145 Seiten. 1976.

Vol. 130: Multiple Criteria Decision Making, Jouy-en-Josas, France. Proceedings 1975. Edited by H. Thiriez and S. Zionts. VI, 409 pages. 1976.

Vol. 131: Mathematical Systems Theory. Proceedings 1975. Edited by G. Marchesini and S. K. Mitter. X, 408 pages. 1976.

Vol. 132: U. H. Funke, Mathematical Models in Marketing. A Collection of Abstracts. XX, 514 pages. 1976.

Vol. 133: Warsaw Fall Seminars in Mathematical Economics 1975. Edited by M. W. Loś, J. Loś, and A. Wieczorek. V. 159 pages. 1976.

Vol. 134: Computing Methods in Applied Sciences and Engineering. Proceedings 1975. VIII, 390 pages. 1976.

Vol. 135: H. Haga, A Disequilibrium – Equilibrium Model with Money and Bonds. A Keynesian – Walrasian Synthesis. VI, 119 pages. 1976.

Vol. 136: E. Kofler und G. Menges, Entscheidungen bei unvollständiger Information. XII, 357 Seiten. 1976.

Vol. 137: R. Wets, Grundlagen Konvexer Optimierung. VI, 146 Seiten. 1976.

Vol. 138: K. Okuguchi, Expectations and Stability in Oligopoly Models. VI, 103 pages. 1976.

Vol. 139: Production Theory and Its Applications. Proceedings. Edited by H. Albach and G. Bergendahl. VIII, 193 pages. 1977.

Vol. 140: W. Eichhorn and J. Voeller, Theory of the Price Index. Fisher's Test Approach and Generalizations. VII, 95 pages. 1976.

Vol. 141: Mathematical Economics and Game Theory. Essays in Honor of Oskar Morgenstern. Edited by R. Henn and O. Moeschlin. XIV, 703 pages. 1977.

Vol. 142: J. S. Lane, On Optimal Population Paths. V, 123 pages. 1977.

Vol. 143: B. Näslund, An Analysis of Economic Size Distributions. XV, 100 pages. 1977.

Vol. 144: Convex Analysis and Its Applications. Proceedings 1976. Edited by A. Auslender. VI, 219 pages. 1977.

Vol. 145: J. Rosenmüller, Extreme Games and Their Solutions. IV, 126 pages. 1977.

Vol. 146: In Search of Economic Indicators. Edited by W. H. Strigel. XVI, 198 pages. 1977.

Vol. 147: Resource Allocation and Division of Space. Proceedings. Edited by T. Fujii and R. Sato. VIII, 184 pages. 1977.

Vol. 148: C. E. Mandl, Simulationstechnik und Simulationsmodelle in den Sozial- und Wirtschaftswissenschaften. IX, 173 Seiten. 1977.

Vol. 149: Stationäre und schrumpfende Bevölkerungen: Demographisches Null- und Negativwachstum in Österreich. Herausgegeben von G. Feichtinger. VI, 262 Seiten. 1977.

Vol. 150: Bauer et al., Supercritical Wing Sections III. VI, 179 pages. 1977.

Vol. 151: C. A. Schneeweiß, Inventory-Production Theory. VI, 116 pages. 1977.

Vol. 152: Kirsch et al., Notwendige Optimalitätsbedingungen und ihre Anwendung. VI, 157 Seiten. 1978.

Vol. 153: Kombinatorische Entscheidungsprobleme: Methoden und Anwendungen. Herausgegeben von T. M. Liebling und M. Rössler. VIII, 206 Seiten. 1978.

Vol. 154: Problems and Instruments of Business Cycle Analysis. Proceedings 1977. Edited by W. H. Strigel. VI, 442 pages. 1978.

Vol. 155: Multiple Criteria Problem Solving. Proceedings 1977. Edited by S. Zionts. VIII, 567 pages. 1978.

Vol. 156: B. Näslund and B. Sellstedt, Neo-Ricardian Theory. With Applications to Some Current Economic Problems. VI, 165 pages. 1978.

continuation on page 155

Lecture Notes in Economics and Mathematical Systems

Managing Editors: M. Beckmann and W. Krelle

263

Martin Schäfer

Resource Extraction and Market Structure

Springer-Verlag
Berlin Heidelberg New York Tokyo

Author

Dr. Martin Schäfer
Universität der Bundeswehr Hamburg
Fachbereich Wirtschafts- und Organisationswissenschaften
Holstenhofweg 85, D-2000 Hamburg 70, FRG

ISBN 978-3-540-16081-6 ISBN 978-3-642-48922-8 (eBook)
DOI 10.1007/978-3-642-48922-8

Library of Congress Cataloging-in-Publication Data. Schäfer, Martin, 1951- Resource extraction and market structure. (Lecture notes in economics and mathematical systems; 263) Bibliography: p. 1. Nonrenewable natural resources–Econometric models. 2. Oligopolies–Econometric models. I. Title. II. Series.
HC59.S344 1986 333.7'0973 86-1786

2142/3140-543210

INTRODUCTION

During the last 15 years the eminent problems of energy scarcity and environmental problems induced many economists to pay closer attention to the questions arising in this area. The question of the effect of the price movement of scarce resources on consumption was analyzed with particular interest. For resources used primarily in production the question of a potential substitute - either as a product or as a new production technology - has to be answered simultaneously.
Again the resource price plays an important role, since research and development towards an alternative technology only makes sense, if the cost of R&D are exceeded by the cost of the respective exhaustible resource.
There are two sides to the problem: On the "demand" side the basic problem is given by determining quantities of an exhaustible resource in order to yield maximal benefit over time. On the "supply" side the owners of the resource are interested in maximizing their profit over time, and thus the rate of supply is determined under this aspect. The two optimal paths, namely for resource extraction and for consumption, do not need to be identical.
Looking at research and development towards an alternative technology the point in time, when this technology will be available, cannot be definitely fixed. The point of the technological breakthrough is influenced by the chosen extraction and/or consumption policies as well as by the cost of developping the new technology. In addition all dependencies among these terms have to be considered. The medium for the control of these variables is obviously given by the resource price. Consequently the structure of the resource market is most important.
Most previous studies analyzing such problems assume either monopolistic or pure competitive markets. However, the markets for most resources or commodities are oligopolistic: In most cases there are only few countries supplying the respective resource deposits or - vice versa - only few countries are the main consumers of these materials. In this monograph we shall also consider resource markets with special consideration of oligopolistic market structures. The general setting will be the microeconomic framework, i.e. macroeconomic influences will not be built into our models.

The first chapter provides a survey of models, using monopolistic or pure competitive market structure. In addition it is assumed that complete information about the size of the resource stock and the demand of the resource is available. In particular Hotelling's r-percent rule will be derived.
Ignoring Hotelling's opinion that future profits must not be discounted, we shall only consider discounted profits of the resource suppliers or discounted utility of the resource users. It is the usual approach to determine the resource value by today's realizable profit. In addition we shall distinguish those resources, which are totally used up in production and those, which can be partially recovered by recycling. In the latter case obviously for total supply the rate of recycling and the extraction rate have to be considered. Recycling obviously depends on the quantity of the resource, already extracted. The dominant approach used is Optimal Control Theory.
In the second chapter some models introducing uncertainty about the size of the resource stock, future technologies, or the cost of developping a substitute for the resource are analyzed. In particular, the cost of research and development towards a backstop technology or the point in time, when this technology will be available, are assumed to be random variables with known probability distribution function. Again there are the same two sides to the problem: The demand side, where future production technologies can make the resource to become "inessential" in the sense that it will no longer be necessary for the production of some consumption good; and the supply side, where we have the problem of an unknown size of the resource stock.
By the third chapter some basic results of the theory of differential games are introduced. The results are used for preparing the subsequent chapters.
The fourth chapter analyzes a representative set of models of duopolistic markets of an exhaustible resource. In particular, price strategies and quantity strategies and open-loop and closed-loop controls are distinguished.
In addition the problem of cartelization of the market and of possible discrete extensions of the continuous analysis are discussed.
The main open analytical problem of this chapter and of the literature in general is the restriction to two oligopolists.
The fifth and final chapter provides our own oligopoly model of a resource market as given by a differential game of more than two play-

ers. This approach allows us to compare with results of the preceding chapters to derive explicit implications for prices, quantities, and the market structure.

The term "solution" will be understood throughout the final chapter as numerically determined open-loop Nash strategies. Cooperation of the suppliers is excluded by assumption.

The algorithm developped and implemented to compute the respective Nash equilibria is a first order gradient algorithm. The numerics are done on a Univac 1100/81.

A sequence of characteristic examples is computed and discussed. They differ with respect to cost structures, time horizons, and initial resource endowments.

On the one hand this monograph is a systematic representation of microeconomic models of resource extraction. On the other hand the monograph presents an oligopoly model and numerical work for more than two oligopolists. It is shown explicitly that analytically almost intractible problems can be advanced numerically.

At this point I would like to thank Prof. Dr. G. Uebe for his permanent readiness to support the progress of this book. Further I am in debt of Prof. Dr. W. Krelle and Prof. Dr. L.F. Pau, who made most valuable and critical suggestions. I have to thank them.

CONTENTS

CHAPTER I 1

DYNAMIC MODELS OF RESOURCE EXTRACTION IN MARKETS OF MONOPOLY OR PURE COMPETITION WITH FULL INFORMATION

1.	Hotelling's Model	1
2.	Optimal Extraction Rates and Exploration	3
2.1	Pure Competition	4
2.2	Monopoly	8
3.	Optimal Extraction Rates and Constant Elasticity of Demand	9
4.	Market Structure and Optimal Depletion Rates	12
4.1	Pure Competition	12
4.2	Monopoly	15
5.	Extraction of an Exhaustible Resource and Production of a Substitute	16
5.1	Social Optimum	17
5.2	Extraction of the Resource and Production of the Substitute by the same Monopoly	18
5.3	Many Owners of the Resource and Production of the Substitute by Monopoly	20
5.4	Many Owners of the Resource and Production of the Substitute by all	22
6.	Extraction of Durable Exhaustible Resources	22
6.1	Discrete Time	22
6.2	Continuous Time	25
6.2.1	Pure Competition	26
6.2.2	Monopoly	28
7.	Conclusions	29

CHAPTER II 31

DYNAMIC MODELS WITH UNCERTAINTY AND MONOPOLISTIC MARKETS OR PURE COMPETITION

1.	Optimal Extraction Rates and Uncertainty with Respect to R&D towards Future Technologies	31
1.1	Exogenous Technical Progress	31

1.1.1 Basic Model 32
1.1.2 First Extension: Production 34
1.1.3 Second Extension: Exhaustible Resources 35
1.1.4 Third Extension: Uncertainty about the Future Technological Development 37
1.2 Endogenous Technical Progress 39
1.2.1 Basic Model 39
1.2.2 Modification of the Basic Model 47
1.2.3 Example with Exponentially Distributed Z 49
2. Optimal Extraction Rates and Unknown Reserves 53
2.1 Monopolistic Extraction Rates Depending on Time only 54
2.2 Monopolistic Extraction Rates Depending on Time and Quantities already Extracted 56
2.3 Optimal Extraction Rates and Pure Competition 58
2.3.1 Basic Model 58
2.3.2 Example with Two Suppliers 58
2.4 Optimal Extraction Rates from Consumer's View 59
2.4.1 Basic Model 59
2.4.2 Example with Exponentially Distributed Z 61
2.5 Pure Competition and Optimal Extraction 61
3. Optimal Extraction Rates and Unknown Costs of the Development of a Substitute 63
3.1 One-period Analysis and Monopoly 63
3.2 One-period Analysis and Pure Competition 66
3.3 Two-period Analysis 67
3.3.1 Optimal Extraction and One Decision Maker 67
3.3.1.1 Basic Model 67
3.3.1.2 Example with Linear Demand 71
3.3.2 Optimal Extraction and Pure Competition 71
3.3.3 Extraction of the Resource and Production of the Substitute by Exactly One Monopoly 73
4. Conclusions 75

CHAPTER III. 77

SHORT INTRODUCTION TO THE THEORY OF DIFFERENTIAL GAMES 77

CHAPTER IV 82

DYNAMIC MODELS OF RESOURCE EXTRACTION AND DUOPOLISTIC MARKETS 82

1. An Introductory Duopoly Model with Production Strategies 83

2. Duopoly with Price Strategies and Exploration 87

2.1 Open-loop Controls 88

2.2 Closed-loop Controls 92

3. A Duopoly Model with Quantity Strategies 96

3.1 Introduction of the Model 96

3.2 Specialization of the Model: Linear-Quadratic Differential Game 98

4. Cartelization and Optimal Extraction of Exhaustible Resources 104

4.1 Pure Competition 104

4.2 Monopolistic Behaviour of the Cartel 106

4.3 Implications of Cartelization to the Profits of the Non-Cartel 109

5. Oligopoly with Discrete Time Parameter 113

6. Conclusions 119

CHAPTER V 121

OLIGOPOLISTIC EXTRACTION WITH CONTINUOUS TIME. 121

1. Basic Model with Quantity Strategies 122

1.1 Introduction of the Model 122

1.2 Algorithm for the Determination of a Nash Equilibrium 125

2. Specializations of the Basic Model 130

2.1 Fixed Resource Stock 130

2.2 Deterministic Expandable Resource Stocks 142

3. Oligopoly and Price Strategies 144

4. Conclusions 148

BIBLIOGRAPHY 150

The notations used throughout in this book are as follows:

x : resource stock,

x^0: Initial size of the resource stock,

q : extraction rate,

p : price,

c : costs,

C : consumption,

K : capital stock,

r : discount rate

J : payoff functional,

$\dot{f}$: derivative of f with respect to time,

f_x: partial derivative of f with respect to x.

I. DYNAMIC MODELS OF RESOURCE EXTRACTION IN MARKETS OF MONOPOLY OR PURE COMPETITION WITH FULL INFORMATION

In this chapter we will discuss some models of the problem of how to sell an exhaustible resource either by exactly one supplier (monopolist) or by many suppliers (pure competition). The objective of all decision makers is to maximize profit over a certain time interval with possibly infinite horizon. All informations about the demand of the resource and its remaining amount are assumed to be given.

I.1 Hotelling's Model

The first attempt to analyze this problem was published by Harold Hotelling (1931). He analyzed which quantities of an extractable resource should be supplied by a mine-owner in order to maximize the present value of the profit.

The extractable quantities at initial time, x^0, are known and the mine-owner's objective is to maximize the functional

$$J = \int_0^\infty p(t)q(t)e^{-rt}dt \ . \tag{1}$$

Here p(t) denotes the price per unit of the resource at time t, q(t) denotes the extraction rate, and r the discount rate. Applying quantity strategies, one has to determine a function $q^*(t)$, which maximizes J, where the price depends on the quantity, supplied at each instant of time.

More precisely, the functional (1) is to be maximized subject to the condition

$$\int_0^\infty q(t)dt = a \leq x^0 . \tag{2}$$

In this model q(t) does not need to be continuous, while $p=p(q(t))$ is assumed to be continuously differentiable in q with $p'(q)<0$ for all $t \in [0,\infty]$. With the demand function

$$p = \frac{1-e^{-kq}}{q}, \tag{3}$$

where k is a positive constant, we find by the calculus of variations the optimal extraction path

$$q^*(t) = \frac{r(\sqrt{(2ka/r)} - t)}{r} .$$

Since p is positive, whenever q is positive, and has a negative first derivative (see equation (3)), p approaches k, as q approaches 0. Moreover, time T of ultimate exhaustion is determined by

$$T = \sqrt{\frac{2ka}{r}}$$

Price strategies are discussed by Hotelling only in relation to pure competitive markets.
Here the solution (i.e. an optimal path p*) is given by discounting the price p^0 at initial time at time t>0. I.e. the price rises according to the discount rate (Hotelling's rule):

$$p(t) = p^0 e^{rt}.$$

The quantity, extracted at time t, is then given by

$$q = f(p;t).$$

Hence we have the equation

$$\int_0^T q(t)dt = \int_0^T f(p^0 e^{rt},t)dt = x^0 ,$$

the upper limit T once again being the time of ultimate exhaustion. This yields

$$f(p^0 e^{rt},t) = 0 \quad \text{for all } t > T.$$

since q will then be zero.
Obviously T depends on the choice of the demand function f.
Choosing e.g.

$$q = e^{-bp}$$

with b constant and q not explicitly dependent on time, the resource will never be exhausted at all. The remaining amount will approach zero only asymptotically.
Both of these models obviously neglect some impacts, which induce the behaviour of extraction paths and/or resource prices: On the one hand extraction costs are neglected. Hence one ignores that it may be more difficult to extract the resource after having exploited a consider-

able big amount so that there are only those deposits left, which require high technical effort for mining.

For instance there is a difference, whether deposits of oil can be exploited just below the ground or whether one hauls it offshore some hundreds of meters below the sea-level, like in the North Sea.

On the other hand the initial amount of the resource is not only known but also fixed. So the possibility of extending the amount available by exploration of further deposits is excluded.

I.2 Optimal Extraction Rates and Exploration

Pindyck (1978) extended Hotelling's model by additional exploration: At initial time a certain amount of the resource stock is known and it is possible to find further deposits of the resource, but only of finite extent; i.e. the resource is still exhaustible. All producers of the resource take quantity strategies, i.e. they choose extraction rates of the stock $x(t)$, which is known at time t, facing the according price, which is given by a demand function.

The extraction costs (=production costs) $c_1(x(t))$ increase with the amount extracted. The known amount of the stock $x(t)$ can be enlarged according to the exploration effort w. The rate of flow of those additions to proven reserves depends on both, exploratory effort w, and cumulative reserve additions y:

$$\dot{y} = f(w,y) \quad \text{with } f_w > 0 \quad \text{and} \quad f_y < 0.$$

The additions increase with the exploratory effort and decline with the increasing amount of additional reserves found before. Hence it follows that further discoveries become increasingly difficult. In addition we implicitly assume that those deposits are exploited first, which can be extracted with least technical effort (see Kemp and Long, 1980b).

The exploration costs, $c_2(w)$, are, corresponding to that assumption, assumed to be increasing in w with

$$c_2(0) = 0 \ , \quad c_2'(w) > 0 \ , \quad c_2'' > 0 \ ,$$

and the marginal discovery costs $c_2(w)/f_w$ are assumed to be increasing

as w increases.
Further we assume for the production cost $c_1(x)$

$$c_1'(x) < 0 \quad \text{and} \quad c_1(x) \to \infty \text{ for } x \to 0. \tag{4}$$

I.2.1 Pure Competition

Each producer (=supplier) of the resource chooses functions $q^*(t)$ so as to maximize

$$J(q,w) = \int_0^T \lfloor qp - c_1(x)q - c_2(w) \rfloor e^{-rt}dt \tag{5}$$

subject to

$$\dot{x} = \dot{y} - q \tag{6}$$

$$\dot{y} = f(w,y) \tag{7}$$

$$x(t) \geq 0, \; q(t) \geq 0, \; w(t) \geq 0. \tag{8}$$

The related Hamiltonian is given by

$$H = qpe^{-rt} - c_1(x)qe^{-rt} - c_2(w)e^{-rt} + \lambda_1(f(w,y)-q) + \lambda_2 f(w,y).$$

Since both, the state equation (6), and the payoff-functional (5) are linear with respect to q, and there are absolute bounds as well as for the resource stock x, the extraction rate q, and the exploratory effort w, there exist, according to the bang-bang principle, optimal controls $q^*(t)$ as follows:

$$q^*(t) = \begin{cases} 0 & \text{if} \quad pe^{-rt} - c_1(x)e^{-rt} - \lambda_1 < 0 \\ \dot{y}(t) - \dot{x}(t) & \phantom{\text{if}} \quad pe^{-rt} - c_1(x)e^{-rt} - \lambda_1 > 0. \end{cases}$$

Since this expression depends on price p, market clearing will always provide that

$$pe^{-rt} - c_1(x)e^{-rt} - \lambda_1 = 0 \,. \tag{9}$$

The multiplier λ_1 can be interpreted as the change of the present value of future profits, resulting from an additional unit of reserves, and can be computed as follows:
Differentiating the Hamiltonian with regard to x and y, we get the Euler-Lagrange equations

$$\dot{\lambda}_1 = -H_x = c_1'(x)q(t)e^{-rt} \quad \text{and} \tag{10}$$

$$\dot{\lambda}_2 = -H_y = -(\lambda_1+\lambda_2)f_y(w,y). \tag{11}$$

Differentiating (9) with respect to time and using (6) and (10) we get

$$\dot{p}(t) = rp(t) - rc_1(x) + c_1(x)f(w,y). \tag{12}$$

Due to (4) the price rises the slower, the more exploratory effort takes place. Moreover, if the production cost would be independent of x, i.e. $c_1'(x)=0$, the price would be uneffected by exploration, and this model would be identical to the basic constant cost model of Hotelling.
Now we can also determine the optimal exploratory effort w* by differentiating the Hamiltonian with respect to w and equating this partial derivative with zero:

$$\frac{\partial H}{\partial w} = -c_2'(w)e^{-rt} + \lambda_1 f_w + \lambda_2 f_w = 0.$$

This yields

$$\lambda_1(t) = \frac{c_2'(w)}{f_w}e^{-rt} - \lambda_2(t). \tag{13}$$

Substituting this equation into (9) and rearranging, we derive

$$\lambda_2(t) = \frac{c_2'(w)}{f_w}e^{-rt} - pe^{-rt} + c_1(x)e^{-rt}, \tag{14}$$

Using (13) and (9) we can rewrite equation (11)

$$\lambda_2(t) = -\frac{f_y}{f_w} \cdot c_2(w)e^{-rt}. \tag{14}$$

On the other hand we get by differentiating equation (8) with respect to time and substitution of equations (6), (7), and (12) for x, y, and p, respectively,

$$\dot{\lambda}_2 = -c_2'(w)\frac{f_{wx} \cdot f}{(f_w)^2}e^{-rt} + \frac{f_w c_2''(w) - c_2'(w) f_{ww}}{(f_w)^2} \cdot \dot{w} e^{-rt} - \tag{15}$$

$$- r\frac{c_2'(w)}{f_w}e^{-rt} - c_1'(x)qe^{-rt}.$$

Equating (15) with (11) and rearranging we derive the equation for the dynamics of the exploratory effort:

$$\dot{w}(t) = \frac{c_2'(w)[(f_{wy}/f_w) \cdot f - f_y + r] + c_1'(x)qf_w}{c_2''(w) - c_2'(w)(f_{ww}/f_w)}. \tag{16}$$

The existence of the right-hand side of this equation can be assured by suitable assumptions on function f with regard to w in the sense that w cannot become arbitrarily large.
Now we have to distinguish between two cases with respect to the boundary conditions for equations (12) and (16):

Case 1:

$$\frac{c_2'(0)}{f_w(0)} = 0:$$

At a certain time T, when ultimate exhaustion of the resource is reached, further exploratory effort is meaningless and hence w=0. As a second boundary condition we have $\lambda_2(T)=0$, since there are no more costs with respect to the cumulative reserves y. Then equation (13) yields

$$p(T) = c_1(x(T)).$$

This equation shows that the price rises and the reserves decrease until the profit, earned by the last remainder of the resource, equals zero.

Moreover, w and q become zero at the same time, i.e. there is no time interval $T_1 < t < T$ with $w(t) = 0$ and $q(t) > 0$. If $w = 0$, then we also have $\lambda_2(t) = 0$ and because of $\lambda_2(T) = 0$ we have $\lambda_2(T_1) = 0$, too. Hence $p(T_1) = c_1(x(T_1))$, and so there is no profit.

Case 2:

$$\frac{c_2'(0)}{f_w(0)} = \phi > 0:$$

Here the exploratory effort vanishes, before q becomes zero. For, suppose $T_1 < T$ denotes the time when w=0, then we get by the transversality conditions $\lambda_2(T)=0$. Once again w=0 yields $\lambda_2=0$ and hence $\lambda_2(T_1)=0$. Hence we have by equations (13) and (9) for $t > T_1$

$$p(t) - c_1(x(t)) = \lambda_1 e^{rt} = \varphi$$

and

$$\dot{\lambda}_1 = -r\lambda_1$$

and with equation (10)

$$c_1'(x(t))q(t) = -r\phi.$$

The behaviour of w, q, and p is given, and w becomes zero at time T_1 with

$$p(t) - c_1(x(t)) \to \varphi \quad , \quad \text{if} \quad t \to T_1$$

and

$$-c_1'(x(t))q(t) \to r\phi \quad , \quad \text{if} \quad t \to T_1 .$$

For $t > T_1$ as well as $p-c_1(x)$ and $c_1'(x)q$ remain constant so that p, c_1, and c_1' increase, whenever q decreases.

I.2.2 Monopoly

Similarly to pure competition the monopolistic producer determines functions q^* and w^* so as to maximize the present value of the profit (1), facing a demand function $p = p(q(t))$ with $p'(q) < 0$. Maximizing the Hamiltonian with respect to q, we have

$$\lambda_1 = (p(t)+q(t)\frac{dp}{dq})e^{-rt} - c_1(x(t))e^{-rt}. \tag{17}$$

Denoting marginal revenue by $E(t) := p(t)+q(t)(dp/dq)$, we get by differentiating (17) with respect to time

$$\dot{\lambda}_1(t) = \dot{E}(t)e^{-rt} - rE(t)e^{-rt} - c_1'(x(t))\dot{x}(t)e^{-rt} + \\ + rc_1(x(t))e^{-rt}. \tag{18}$$

Equating this with (10) we have

$$\dot{E}(t)-rE(t)-c_1'(x(t))f(w,y)+rc_1(x(t)) = c_1'(x(t))q(t) \tag{19}$$

and this gives us the dynamics of marginal revenue

$$\dot{E}(t) = rE(t) - rc_1(x(t)) + c_1'(x(t))f(w,y) + c_1'(x(t))q(t).$$

Parallel to the competitive market situation the marginal revenue of the monopolistic producer rises according to the discount factor r, provided the extraction costs are independent of the remaining reserves, i.e. if c_1 is constant and consequently $c_1' = 0$. Analogous to the case of pure competition we derive by maximization of the Hamiltonian with respect to w the same dynamics of the exploratory effort as (16):

$$\dot{w}(t) = \frac{c_2'(w)\lfloor(f_{wy}/f_w)f-f_y+r\rfloor+c_1'(x)qf_w}{c_2''(w)-c_2'(w)(f_{ww}/f_w)}. \tag{16$'$}$$

However, the solution $w^*(t)$ in the monopolistic case differs from the competitive case. As long as the extraction rate q of the monopolistic producer is smaller than that one of the competitor, w is greater,

since $c' < 0$. This implies that the exploratory effort of the monopolistic producer is initially smaller and is greater at the end of the time interval, than for the competitive suppliers.
In the preceding model the dynamics of the price depend on the amount of the initially known resource stock. If it is so big that the corresponding extraction costs are low enough, then the price increases slowly during the whole time interval, according to Hotelling's rule. Otherwise, if the initially known amount of the resource is small, extraction costs are high and so is the price. After this it declines according to the additional reserves, found by greater exploratory effort, and increases again, when the total reserves approach ultimate exhaustion: the price curve is U-shaped.

I.3 Optimal Extraction Rates and Constant Elasticity of Demand

A model, stressing elasticity of demand and, similar Pindyck's, dealing with monopolistic and competitive market structure was discussed by J. Stiglitz (1976). Stiglitz showed that for specific assumptions, different to those of section I.2, the competitive market equilibrium is identical to optimal patterns of monopolistic market. The demand function is assumed to be log-linear:

$$p = f(t)q^{\alpha-1} \quad \text{with } 0 < \alpha < 1 \,. \tag{20}$$

Function $f \neq 0$ can be interpreted as developments of the price due to external influences, autonomous of q.
Obviously the elasticity of demand is constant and equals $1/(1-\alpha)$.
The monopolistic producer now faces the standard optimization problem (1) and (2).
Substituting (20) into (1) and introducing the Lagrange multiplier λ on the constraint (2), we get the problem of maximizing

$$\int_0^\infty [f(t)q^{\alpha}e^{-rt}-\lambda q]dt.$$

That means that we choose extraction rates $q(t)$ such that

$$\alpha f(t)q^{\alpha-1}(t)e^{-rt}-\lambda = 0 \quad \text{holds.}$$

Substituting again (20) we have

$$\alpha e^{-rt}p(t) - \lambda = 0$$

and by logarithmic differentiation

$$\dot{p}/p = r \quad \Rightarrow \quad \dot{p}(t) = rp(t). \tag{21}$$

This result is just Hotelling's rule with respect to competitive market: the price rises according to the discount rate.
Once again applying (20), i.e. solving for q, we derive the optimal depletion rate

$$\frac{\dot{q}}{q} = \frac{r-(f'/f)}{\alpha-1} \quad \Rightarrow \quad \dot{q}(t) = \frac{r-(f'(t)/f(t))}{\alpha-1}q(t).$$

Both, price and depletion path, apply in the cases of monopolistic and competitive market structure equally. Moreover, we have $q(t)>0$ due to constant elasticity of demand and since $f(t)>0$. I.e. the resource will be completely depleted only asymptotically.
Subsequently we drop the assumption of zero extraction costs and assume costs, which are constant per unit, yet decreasing with time. This assumption may not appear plausible, in particular with respect to resource exhaustibility.
The profit of the monopolistic producer is

$$\int_0^\infty (fq^\alpha - cq)e^{-rt}dt$$

and with respect to the profit maximum we have

$$e^{-rt}(\alpha f(t)q^{\alpha-1}(t)-c(t))-\lambda = 0 .$$

As above, we get a differential equation for the price p:

$$(\dot{p}/p) = r(1-\gamma_m) + (\dot{c}/c)\gamma_m \quad \text{with} \quad \gamma_m = \frac{c(t)}{\alpha p(t)}. \tag{22}$$

Obviously price can decrease, if extraction costs decline rapidly.
Analogous we derive in the case of competition

$$(\dot{p}/p) = r(1-\gamma_w) + (\dot{c}/c)\gamma_w \quad \text{where} \quad \gamma_w = c/p . \tag{21'}$$

If p is identical for both cases, monopoly and competition, the inequality $\gamma_w(t) > \gamma_m(t)$ applies and hence $\dot{p}/p$ is greater in the competitive case. Consequently the price curves can cross one another only once a time, and the monopolistic producer initially supplies less, and his price is higher for small t than it is in competition. This yields that monopoly price will be lower, when ultimate exhaustion will be approached. I.e. the later generations profit by higher prices now. However, the monopolistic equilibrium is not efficient. Assuming now - more realistically - that costs increase with time, we once again get the equation

$$\frac{\dot{p}}{p} = r(1-\frac{c(t)}{\alpha p(t)}) + \frac{\dot{c}(t)}{\alpha p(t)} \qquad (21)''$$

or, equivalently,

$$\dot{p}(t) = rp(t) - (1/\alpha)(c(t) - \dot{c}(t))$$

The price patterns depend on how rapidly the cost will rise, and consequently we have to distinguish between the following two cases:

1. $c(t) - \dot{c}(t) < 0$:
   Here we have

$$\dot{p}(t) = rp(t) - (1/\alpha)(c(t)-\dot{c}(t)) > 0 \quad \text{for all t.}$$

2. $c(t) - \dot{c}(t) > 0$:
   Here we have

$$\dot{p}(t) = rp(t) - (1/\alpha)(c(t)-\dot{c}(t) < 0 \quad \text{if, and only if}$$

$$\dot{c}(t) < c(t) - \alpha rp(t) \quad \text{holds.}$$

Obviously the price path depends on level and increase of costs. Moreover, the following condition must be satisfied:

$$0 < \alpha rp(t) < c(t)-\dot{c}(t)$$

By this inequality we can see that (with constant increase of costs) the price will rise damped proportional to the costs.

A defect of this analysis could be that the extraction costs do not depend explicitly on the remaining resource stock.

I.4 Market Structure and Optimal Depletion Rates

Until now we have discussed, how to extract a fixed stock of a resource with regard to constant elasticity of demand and to the possibility of finding and extracting further initially unexplored reserves. The amount of those initially unexplored reserves was assumed to be finite. Furthermore the actually explored and depleted amount was dependent on the exploration costs. Moreover, it was found that the time patterns of price and extraction in the monopolistic case may possibly equal those in pure competition. Now the implications of the market structure will be discussed more detailed.
We distinguish optimal patterns and patterns determined by market force. We once again assume that there is a fixed and finite resource stock, which can be exploited with certain costs. Since this stock is finite, the part remaining for later use depends on the amount extracted. Each deposit is assumed to be controlled by exactly one decision maker and there is a pure competitive market. I.e. each decision maker sets his price of the resource so as to maximize discounted profit by selling his part of the total resource stock. Suppose, x_i^0 denotes the quantity available at initial time to the i-th supplier, and $q_i(t)$ denotes his extraction rate depending only on time. Then once again constraint (2) applies. The extraction costs $c_i(q_i(t))$ depend on the extraction rate and (not necessarily) on time. This cost function serves as a certain measure for the quality of the deposit. If the values of the cost function are high, then reserves can only be extracted with high technical effort. Moreover, it is assumed that the marginal extraction cost $\partial c_i/\partial q_i$ are strictly increasing with respect to q_i, i.e c_i is strictly convex in q_i.

I.4.1 Pure Competition

Assume that the resource is sold with price p(t) and p(t) depends <u>only</u> on time and does <u>not</u> depend on the extraction rate. If the owner of the i-th deposit wishes to maximize his profit, he has to solve the optimization problem

$$\int_0^\infty [p(t)q_i(t) - c_i(q_i(t),t)]e^{-rt}dt \rightarrow \max$$

subject to constraint (2).

Then we get the Lagrangians

$$L_i = \int_0^\infty [p(t)q_i(t)-c_i(q_i(t),t)]e^{-rt}dt + \lambda_i(x_i^0-\int_0^\infty q_i(t)dt). \qquad (23)$$

The multipliers λ_i have to satisfy the conditions

$$\lambda_i \geq 0 \quad \text{and} \quad (\int_0^\infty q_i(t)dt-x_i^0)\lambda_i = 0 \ ;$$

i.e. either $\lambda_i=0$ or constraint (2) is binding.
By the Kuhn-Tucker Theorem we derive the necessary conditions

$$(p(t) - \frac{\partial c_i}{\partial q_i}(q_i^*(t),t)) - \lambda_i e^{rt} \begin{cases} =0 & , q_i^*(t)>0 \\ \leq 0 & , q_i^*(t)=0. \end{cases} \qquad (24)$$

If

$$\int_0^\infty q_i(t)dt = x_i^0 \ ,$$

then $\lambda_i>0$ holds, and price and marginal costs are different; if in this case the resource will be extracted optimally, the marginal costs must be lower than the price. Interpreting the expression $\lambda_i e^{rt}$ as opportunity costs, λ_i is the present value of those opportunity costs. Then - by the necessary condition for an optimal extraction path - the marginal unit cost of extraction plus the additional opportunity cost must equal the price of the resource.
Furthermore, if the initial amounts of the deposits are distinct, then the extraction paths due to distinct deposits can never cross each other. At each point of time the extraction path of the bigger reserve will be higher than the extraction path of the smaller reserve. Moreover, an optimal depletion rate can be zero initially, increase after some time, and finally decline to zero, when ultimate exhaustion of the deposit will be reached.
If the extraction costs are convex in q_i, then the necessary condition (24) is sufficient, too. If c_i is strictly convex, then $q_i^*(t)$ is even unique.
Since pure competition is assumed, we get the total extraction path

$$Q(t) = \sum_{i=1}^{N} q_i^*(t) \ ,$$

and from the demand function we derive the price path

$$p(t) = p(Q(t);t).$$

An allocation, where all $q_i^*(t)$ solve the optimization problem above, i.e. do satisfy (24), and where we have this price path, is called an equilibrium.

Now we have to distinguish three cases:

1. Zero Marginal Costs:
   The extraction rates are chosen so that the corresponding price rises proportional to the discount rate (Hotelling's rule).
2. Constant Marginal Costs:
   Marginal costs are equal for all suppliers, but the initial endowments are different and consequently the extraction costs are also different:
   The price path is composed of different curves of the form $c_i+\lambda_i e^{rt}$. The deposits will be exploited one after another and the succession will correspond to the increasing costs, i.e. the next expensive deposit will be exploited starting at the point of time, when the preceding one will be totally exhausted. Obviously, constant extraction costs for each deposit are assumed. The rate of price increase is always below the discount rate.
3. Increasing marginal costs:
   Different deposits have different extraction costs, but each cost function is different from each other only by a multiplicative scaling factor. Now several deposits will be extracted simultaneously, and the extraction rate depends on the corresponding initial endowment x_i^0. The greater the initial endowment the greater will be the extraction rate and the higher will be the marginal costs along an optimal extraction path.

I.4.2 Monopoly

The monopolistic supplier, who is the owner of all reserves, solves the optimization problem

$$\int_0^\infty \sum_{i=1}^{N} (p(Q(t),t)q_i(t) - c_i(q_i(t),t))e^{-rt}dt \quad \to \quad \max \tag{25}$$

subject to constraint (2) and

$$Q(t) = \sum_{i=1}^{N} q_i(t). \tag{26}$$

Analogous to the competitive case we have the necessary conditions

$$p(Q(t),t) + Q(t)\frac{\partial p}{\partial Q} - \frac{\partial c_i}{\partial q_i} - \lambda_i e^{rt} \begin{cases} = 0 & , q_i>0 \\ \leq 0 & , q_i=0. \end{cases}$$

Denoting the marginal revenue by

$$E(t) := p(t) + Q(t)\frac{dp}{dQ} \tag{27}$$

we have the following two propositions about ultimate exhaustion of the resource (Sweeney, 1977):

1. Suppose, in the competitive case ultimate exhaustion is reached at time τ. If the demand function is continuous with respect to t and Q at the point Q=0, then ultimate exhaustion will in the monopolistic case will not be reached at time τ.

2. Suppose,

   $$\frac{\partial E}{\partial Q} < 0 \quad \text{and} \quad \frac{\partial E}{\partial t} \leq rE \quad \text{hold.}$$

   Then the extraction rate, chosen by a monopolistic supplier, is not greater than the extraction rate due to competition, provided the elasticity of demand is non-decreasing with time.
   Moreover, if the cost functions decrease over time, then the monopolistic supplier will exploit a fixed resource stock slower than it will be done in the case of competition.

I.5 Extraction of an Exhaustible Resource and Production of a Substitute

Corresponding to I.2, where the size of the initially known resource stock could be enlarged by exploration, we will now discuss a model, dealing with the possibility of producing a fully substitutive good for the resource. The production costs per unit of the substitute depend on the state of technology, which always is assumed to be given, and can be improved by research and development. The extraction costs of the resource are assumed to be constant (see Vousden (1977) and Kemp and Long (1982)).

Suppose, the initial amount of the resource, x^0, is known and fixed and depleteable at constant costs k per unit so that these costs accumulate to kq(t) at time t, where q(t) denotes once again the extraction rate.

A full substitute can be produced with costs c=c(R,y), where y denotes the production and R represents the state of technology. Expenditure on research and development will be denoted by $g(\rho)$ ($\rho = dR/dt$). The total revenue by selling the resource and the substitute is given by $\pi(q+y) =: \pi(z)$ and hence we have the average revenue

$$p(z) = \frac{\pi(z)}{z}.$$

With this notation we have the optimization problem

$$\int_0^\infty \lfloor u(q+y)-kq-c(R,y)-g(\rho)\rfloor e^{-rt}dt \to \max_{q,y,\rho} \tag{28}$$

subject to

$$\begin{aligned} &\frac{dx}{dt} = -q(t) \;, \quad x(0) = x^0 > 0 \;, \quad \lim_{t\to\infty} x(t) \geq 0 \\ &\dot{R} = \rho \;, \quad R(0) = R^0 \;, \quad q,y,\rho > 0. \end{aligned} \tag{29}$$

The utility function u is given by

$$u(q+y) =: u(z) = \int_0^z p(\zeta)d\zeta.$$

Further we assume that all functions are twice differentiable and c(R,y) is convex.

Using the Lagrangean

$$L = u(q+y) - kq - c(R,y) - g(\rho) - \lambda_1 q + \lambda_2 \rho$$

we can derive the well-known necessary conditions for a maximum of the objective functional (28).

I.5.1 Social Optimum.

Define z^s by

$$u'(z^s) = p(z^s) = k,$$

R^s by

$$c_y(R^s, z^s) = k,$$

$y^s(R)$ by

$$c_y(R, y^s) = p(y^s),$$

$p^s(R)$ by

$$p^s = p(y^s),$$

and R^{s^*} by

$$-c_R(R^{s^*}, y^s(R^{s^*}))/r = g'(0).$$

It can be shown that R^{s^*} is unique, if it exists. On the social optimum we have the following

<u>Proposition (Kemp and Long (1982)):</u>

a) If $R^0 > R^s$, then $q(t) \equiv 0$ is optimal.

b) if $R^0 < R^s$, then either
   (i) $z(t) > z^s$ for all t, and p(z) never increases, or
   (ii) $z(0) < z^s$ and p(z) increases until the resource stock is exhausted and thereafter p(z) is non-increasing.

c) After the resource stock will have been exhausted, $y^s(R)$ will be the optimal production rate, if it exists. If it does not exist, then the optimal output equals zero. If optimal output is positive, then it is increasing with respect to R.

d) Investment in R&D to ensure better production technologies will be optimal, if

$$-c_R(R^0, y^s(R^0))/r > g'(0).$$

There will be no investment after time t, if and only if $R(t) > R^{s*}$. There can be investment into R&D, before production of the substitute begins.

Subsequently we will discuss this model with respect to different market structures.

I.5.2 Extraction of the Resource <u>and</u> Production of the Substitute by the Same Monopoly

Suppose, the extraction of the resource and the production of the substitute is controlled by exactly one monopolistic supplier.
As above, we define
z^m by

$$\pi'(z^m) = k,$$

R^m by

$$c_y(R^m, z^m) = k,$$

$y^m(R)$ by

$$c_y(R, y^m) = \pi'(y^m),$$

$p^m(R)$ by

$$p^m = p(y^m),$$

and finally R^{m*} by

$$-c_R(R^{m*}, y^m(R^{m*}))/r = g'(0).$$

In this case it can be shown, too, that R^{m*} is unique, if it exists. On the optimal policies of a monopolistic supplier we have the following

Proposition (Kemp and Long (1982)):

a) If $R^0 > R^m$, then $q(t) \equiv 0$ is optimal.
b) If $R^0 < R^m$, then either
   (i) $z(t) > z^m$ for all t and $\pi'(z)$ never increases, or
   (ii) $z(0) < z^m$ and $\pi'(z)$ increases, until the resource stock will be exhausted, and thereafter $\pi'(z)$ is non-increasing.
c) After the resource stock will have been exhausted, $y^m(R)$ will be the optimal production rate of the substitute, if it exists. If it does not exist, the optimal output y equals zero. If it is positive, $y^m(R)$ is increasing with respect to R.
d) It is optimal to invest in R&D towards a better production technology, if

$$-c_R(R^0, y^m(R^0))/r > g'(0).$$

There will be no investment after time t, if and only if $R(t) > R^{m*}$. Investment in R&D can take place, before production of the substitute begins.

A comparism of the two propositions, which coincide almost word by word, yields the following relations (Kemp and Long, 1982):

Proposition (Kemp and Long, 1982):

a) $z^s > z^m$;
b) $R^s > R^m$, if $c_{yy} > 0$ and
   $R^s = R^m$, if $c_{yy} = 0$;
c) $R^{s*} > R^{m*}$.

In other words: A resource stock is socially valuable but worthless for a monopolist, if $R^s > R^0 > R^m$; i.e the monopolist overconserves to the point of never using the resource. On the other hand, if $R^{s*} > R^0 > R^{m*}$, it is socially optimal to eventually invest in R&D, but suboptimal for the monopolist to do so.

I.5.3 Many Owners of the Resource and Production of the Substitute by Monopoly

Now we will discuss optimal policies for the case that there are many suppliers of the resource but only exactly one producer of the substitute.

Suppose, the monopolist will buy the whole resource stock available at price $p^0 - k$, i.e. we have to solve the problem

$$\int_0^\infty \left[\pi(q+y) - kq - c(R,y) - g(\rho)\right] e^{-rt} dt - p^0 x^0 \to \max$$

subject to the constraints

$$\dot{x} = -q \ , \quad x(0) = x^0 \ , \quad \lim_{t\to\infty} x(t) \geq 0$$

$$\dot{R} = \rho \ , \quad R(0) = R^0$$

$$\frac{\dot{p}}{p-k} \leq \rho \ , \quad q, y, \rho, p^0 \geq 0.$$

In order to exclude the trivial case that the resource stock is worthless, suppose, $\rho = 0$ along the optimal path.

Then we still have to distinguish three cases, corresponding to the relative values of R^0, R^s, and R^m.

<u>Case 1</u> ($R^0 \geq R^s$):

$c_y(R^0, y^m(R^0)) \leq k$.

The resource stock is worthless for the monopolist, since it is cheaper for him to produce the substitute. But for the "little" owners of the resource deposits it is a certain threat potential. So it is optimal for the monopolist to buy the total stock at the price $p^0 - k$, $p^0 \leq p^m(R^0)$, and then to produce the substitute only. Until the time, when $p^m(R^0)$ is reached, the price of the substitute rises, beginning at p^0 according to the differential equation

$$\dot{p} = r(p-k).$$

From this time on the price will remain constant at p^m. For the optimal initial price p^{0*} it can be shown (see Kemp and Long (1982)) that it lies between the extraction cost k and the price p^m due to monopolistic extraction:

$$k < p^{0*} < pm.$$

Case 2 ($R^0 < R^m$):

Here we have to distinguish two subcases:

a) $c_y(R^0,0) > k$:

The optimal policy is composed by three subsequent phases: During the first phase, the market will be satisfied only by extracting the resource, and the price develops according to the equation

$$\dot{p} = r(p-k).$$

At the end of this phase the resource stock will be totally depleted. In the subsequent phase only the substitute will be supplied, and price development is described by the same differential equation. In the third phase, finally, the price of the substitute will be constantly p^m.

b) $c_y(R^0,0) < k$:

During the first phase, different to subcase a), the substitute is supplied in addition to the resource. Phases 2 and 3 agree with those of subcase a).

Case 3 ($R^m < R^0 < R^s$):

Principally optimal policies coincide with those ones of case 1. However, there can be a difference, i.e. initially we have the following:

Let $\bar{y}$ be defined by

$$c_y(R^0,\bar{y}) = k$$

and $\bar{p}$ by

$$\bar{p} = p(\bar{y}),$$

then we have $\bar{p}>k$, since $R^0<R^s$.

Now suppose, $\bar{p}>p^0$: Then the monopolist is interested in selling more than $\bar{y}$ during a period, beginning at initial time. I.e. extraction of the resource takes place, too, until $p=\bar{p}$. From then on, a regime corresponding to case 1 applies.

I.5.4 Many Owners of the Resource and Production of the Substitute by All

If, finally, not only the extraction of the resource, but also the production of the substitute as well as R&D towards a corresponding production technology are controlled by many decision makers, we derive the following results:
If the price of the whole resource stock equals p^*-k with p^* defined analogously to p above, and if

$$p^*-k < p^m(R^0)-k \quad \text{holds,}$$

then we have the same policies as in I.5.3. But, if $p^* > p^m(R^0)$, then there is initially no phase with increasing price. If strict inequality holds, then the price patterns start in jumping from p^* down to $p^m(R^0)$.

I.6 Extraction of Durable Exhaustible Resources

So far there has been one type of resource only. However, different resources can have different qualities, which influence the use in production and consequently its depletion.
Now we discuss some problems for extracting an exhaustible resource, which can be used in production for several times by recycling; i.e. we will analyze a durable exhaustible resource.
A certain quantity of a resource just extracted may be profitable for the moment, yet diminishe its future sales prospects.

I.6.1 Discrete Time

Assume that a monopolist can control the extraction of a durable exhaustible resource, and his objective is to maximize the present value of the profit, during n periods of time. The monopolist makes his decisions about the quantities, to be extracted, always at the beginning of a period, i.e. we have a discrete time model.
The decision refers to the quantity of the resource, which will be extracted during this period, and should be sold at the end of this period.

The discounted profit, earned by the output of the i-th period, is given by

$$r^i\pi_i := r^i q_i(p_i - c).$$

The notation used is basically unchanged. Index i denotes the period of time. The extraction costs c are assumed to be constant. Then the monopolist's objective is to maximize the functional

$$\sum_{i=1}^{n} r^i \pi_i = \sum_{i=1}^{n} r^i q_i(p_i - c) \tag{30}$$

subject to

$$\sum_{i=1}^{n} q_i \leq x^0. \tag{2)'$$

Durability of the resource means that the output of one period can be held in use more than n periods. Hence price p_i of period i depends on the output of all preceding periods:

$$p_i = f_i(q_1, \ldots, q_i)$$

Hence the price function generally is different during different periods.
With regard to (2)' we get the Lagrangean

$$L = \sum_{i=1}^{n} r^i q_i(p_i - c) + \lambda(x^0 - \sum_{i=1}^{n} q_i),$$

where x^0 denotes the amount of the resource stock, known at the beginning of the first period.
The necessary condition, which has to be satisfied by an optimal price, is

$$E_i - c = r(p_{i+1} - c), \quad i<n \tag{31}$$

where E_i denotes marginal revenue with respect to price p_i.
The left-hand side describes the increase of the profit, which can be earned by a marginal increase of the production during the i-th period; the right-hand side can be interpreted as the opportunity cost, related to this increase of resource output.

In the case of pure competition we have $E_i = p_i$, and an optimal extraction policy causes that net price p-c rises according to the discount rate. This, however, is precisely Hotelling's result, which was obtained without considering the durability of the resource. Now we modify this simple model by taking into consideration uncertainty with respect to future demand: The price of the resource during the i-th period now is assumed to be a function of cumulative outputs of all preceding periods and a random variable, which gives the decision maker's subjective assumption with regard to future demand:

$$p_i = g_i(Q_i, v_i),$$

where

$$Q_i = \sum_{j=1}^{i} q_j$$

and v_i denotes a random variable.
Then we have the optimization problem of maximizing the expected profits

$$E(\sum_{i=1}^{n} r^i \pi_i) \qquad (30)'$$

Here we get the necessary condition, analogous to (32)

$$E_i - c = r(p_{i+1} - c) \quad , \quad i < n . \qquad (31)'$$

Obviously, the decision regarding the quantities to be extracted depend on the probability distribution of v_i.
Another modification of this model could be a more sophisticated consideration of the topic "durability" of a resource. Precious gems, e.g., almost never wear out, while e.g. steel rusts and can be used further only in parts by recycling. I.e. a certain part is lost. Once again one gets necessary conditions for an optimal policy analogous to (31) and (31)'. In summary we can obtain the following result:

<u>Proposition (Stewart (1980)):</u>
If the market of an exhaustible resource is purely competitive, net price of the resource rises according to the discount rate, independent from whether the resource is durable or not.

If the market is not perfect, the price rises again proportional to the discount rate, if the resource is not durable; if it is durable, the marginal revenue of the i-th period equals discounted profit margin of the subsequent period. This policy leads to a decreasing price over time. The price pattern of commodities with limited durability will be between those two extremals in dependence of the recycling rate.

I.6.2 Continuous Time

The result of I.6.1 contains the following shortcoming: Hotelling's r-percent rule does not necessarily apply in the case of a durable good. Assuming constant demand, the cumulative extracted quantity of the resource can only increase - with constant extraction costs - so that the price can only decline. The misdirection of Stewart's assumptions lies first in the assumption of constant extraction costs; it implies that the extraction rate initially must be infinite. Secondly, the demand is a relation of the quantity of the resource being in circulation;

$$D(Q) = f(Q)y(t) , \quad f'(Q) < 0 \tag{32}$$

where y(t) denotes an autonomous increase of the demand, e.g.

$$y(t) = e^{\alpha t}.$$

The term D(Q) denotes the marginal value of the quantity of the resource, being in circulation. The cost of use of one unit of the resource are given by

$$rp - \dot{p} + \delta p , \tag{33}$$

where $1-\delta$ denotes the rate of recycling of the circulating quantity of the resource.
Equating (33) and D(Q) we obtain the following price dynamics

$$\dot{p} = -f(Q)e^{\alpha t} + (r+\delta)p. \tag{34}$$

Obviously we assumed that future development of the market is known.

Then the optimization problem of a monopolistic supplier is given by

$$\int_0^{\infty}(pq-c(q))e^{-rt}dt \rightarrow \max_q \qquad (35)$$

subject to (34) and

$$\dot{Q} = q - \delta Q , \quad Q(0) = 0 , \qquad (36)$$

$$\dot{R} = q , \quad Q \leq x^0 , \quad q \geq 0 . \qquad (37)$$

R denotes the cumulative extracted quantity corresponding to the extraction rate q, and x^0 denotes, as usually, the initial amount of the whole resource stock.

I.6.2.1 Pure Competition

In perfect competition no single producer can control the price p and the circulating quantity of the extracted resource, Q. Hence there is the optimization problem (35) subject to (37). Taking into account the conditions (34) and (36) we can determine price and extraction paths conformal to the market by use of the following Hamiltonian

$$H = (pq - c(q))e^{-rt} - \lambda q. \qquad (38)$$

The necessary condition for a maximum is

$$\lambda = (p - c'(q))e^{-rt}. \qquad (39)$$

To determine the corresponding price pattern we use the demand relation (32). For, differentiating (39) with respect to time and equating the derivative with zero, we get the differential equation for the extraction rate

$$\dot{q} = (1/c''(q))(\dot{p} - rp + rc'(q))$$

and by (34)

$$\dot{q} = (1/c''(q))(\delta p + rc'(q) - f(Q)e^{\alpha t}). \qquad (40)$$

Since this differential equation depends on the price and the circulating resource quantity, it has to be solved simultaneously with the equations (34) and (36) subject to the boundary conditions

$$Q(0) = 0 \,, \quad q(T) = 0 \quad \text{and} \quad \int_0^T q(t)dt = x^0 . \tag{41}$$

I.e. T denotes the time of ultimate exhaustion.
We discuss the solution of this problem with respect to three subcases:

1. Unrestricted recycling, static demand ($\delta=\alpha=0$):
   Equation (40) collapses into

$$\dot{q} = -(f(Q) - rc'(q))/c''(q). \tag{40)'$$

   Obviously the extraction rate q can be different from zero, only if $f(Q)/r>c'(q)$; i.e. capitalized marginal flow of the unit value of the resource is greater than the marginal extraction costs of this unit. Hence $q > 0$ until time T is reached. The price declines with time.

2. Restricted recycling, static demand ($\delta>0$, $\alpha=0$):
   Equation (40) specializes into

$$\dot{q} = -(f(Q) - rc'(q) - \delta p)/c''(q). \tag{40)''$$

   By equation (34) we see that the price decreases, if

$$\int_0^T q(t)dt < x^0 \quad \text{for all } T < \infty .$$

   Here we have a monotonically decreasing extraction rate, approaching asymptotically the value $\delta\tilde{Q}$, while Q approaches monotonically increasing the value $\tilde{Q}$. Price p approaches a corresponding price level $\tilde{p}$. If the resource is bounded, i.e. it will be totally exhausted at some time T, then q declines down to zero. Cumulative amount R increases until a certain point of time, T_1, is reached, where

$$q = \delta Q(T_1).$$

   From time T_1 on Q decreases monotonically and approaches asymptotically zero. In other words: the price path is U-shaped.

3. The arbitrary case ($\delta>0$, $\alpha>0$):
The extraction rate is given by equation (40) in general. Extraction patterns are similar to those of the second case, although production of the resource starts at a lower level. If ultimate exhaustion will never be reached, then the price equals the marginal costs and as well as q and Q approach asymptotically the constants $\delta\tilde{Q}$ and $\tilde{Q}$, respectively. Since q increases along that path, the price moves along the curve of the marginal costs. If the resource is bounded, i.e. there exists a point in time, T, with

$$\int_0^T q(t)dt = x^0,$$

then q again approaches monotonically decreasing 0 and Q initially increases and thereafter decreases.
Hence due to q and Q the price path is U-shaped, if α is small enough. However, if α is relatively great (yet $\alpha < r$) then it is possible that the price can increase monotonically. It can even be increasing strictly monotonically, since Q approaches zero only asymptotically for $t > T$.
If $\alpha > r$, then there is no extraction at all, since the present value of the resource can be enlarged by shifting the extraction.

I.6.2.2 Monopoly

If there is a monopolistic market structure, we get by (33), (36), and (37) the Hamiltonian

$$\begin{aligned} H = (pq - c(q))e^{-rt} - \lambda_1 q - \lambda_2(q - \delta R) - \\ - \lambda_3(-f(R)e^{\alpha t} + (r+\delta)p). \end{aligned} \tag{42}$$

Maximizing (42) with respect to q, we derive the revenue

$$(p - c'(q))e^{-rt} = (\lambda_1 + \lambda_2). \tag{39'}$$

Revenue only increases with the discount rate r, if $(\dot{\lambda}_1+\dot{\lambda}_2)=0$.
On the other hand

$$\dot{\lambda}_1 = -\frac{\partial H}{\partial R} = 0 ,$$

$$\dot{\lambda}_2 = -\frac{\partial H}{\partial Q} = -\delta\lambda_2 - \lambda_3 f'(Q) ,$$

and

$$\dot{\lambda}_3 = -\frac{\partial H}{\partial p} = -qe^{-rt} + (r+\delta)\lambda_3$$

hold.

Consequently, $\dot{\lambda}_2=0$ holds, only if $\lambda_3 f'(Q)$ is constant with respect to time. Since this must apply for each function f(Q), it has to be true, if $f''(Q)=0$. But then λ_3 has to be constant, according to the Hamiltonian (42), and thus qe^{-rt} will be constant. But since q finally decreases we have $\dot{\lambda}_3 \neq 0$ and consequently $\dot{\lambda}_2 \neq 0$. Hence the revenue cannot rise with the discount rate r. I.e. in this case Hotelling's rule does not apply.

I.7 Conclusions

In this chapter some basic models of resource extraction plus exploration are discussed. Significant issues are the structure of the demand function, production of a substitute, and the impacts due to the grade of durability of the resource. Starting with Hotelling's model, we derive optimal price and extraction patterns related to monopolistic markets and to pure competition. Due to the different additional assumptions those optimal paths may possibly differ from Hotelling's rule.

E.g. in the case of exploration we have found the price increases according to Hotelling's rule only, if the initial amount of the resource is big enough. Otherwise, i.e. if the initially known resource stock is relatively small and consequently the extraction costs, depending on the size of the stock are high, the initial price of the resource will be high, too. The price declines, since further deposits will be explored and consequently the resource stock available grows. Finally the price rises again, when ultimate exhaustion is reached. In the case of constant elasticity of demand, however, again without considering extraction costs, precisely Hotelling's rule can be obtained. In this case the resource will be exhausted only asymptotically.

Yet if extraction costs depending only on time are used, the Hotelling property vanishes: If extraction costs decrease rapidly, the price can also decrease.

Moreover, conservation depends on the market structure: The monopolist exploits his reserves more conservatively than pure competition.

If extraction costs increase with time, the price can decrease only, if the increase of costs is smaller than the difference between the costs and the price, weighted by the discount factor and the exponent of the log-linear demand function.

Otherwise Hotelling's rule again applies.

The same result can be obtained, if the extraction costs depend on time <u>and</u> on the extraction rate. Moreover, in this case the monopolist extracts his reserves slower than extraction takes place in competition.

I.e. the validity of Hotelling's rule depends crucially on the cost structure: If the costs are not constant, it does not apply or it has to be modified in the sense that the price changes are only proportional to the discount rate.

For the (deterministic) production of a substitutive good, the state of technology in relation to extraction will be dominant. If the technology is advanced enough initially, then there will be no extraction at all.

Again monopolistic production of the resource and the substitute will be lower than in the competitive case.

In the case of durable exhaustible resources, the precise definition of durability is important. The concept used is related to recycling. If the rate of recycling is arbitrarily large, i.e. the total resource will be available again and again - the resource is perfectly durable - Hotelling's r-percent rule fails again.

II. DYNAMIC MODELS WITH UNCERTAINTY AND MONOPOLISTIC MARKETS OR PURE COMPETITION

After discussion of durable and non-durable exhaustible resources, we shall now turn to aspects of risk and uncertainty. Until now the total initial amount of the resource has been known by assumption and the dynamics for exploration and for research and development towards a substitution technology were assumed to be known.
However, the assumption of perfect foresight with respect to use and extraction of an exhaustible resource is dubious. Knowledge of all future technical progress is assumed.
Since different resources are not equally necessary for the production of a consumption good, we only consider those, which are "essential" in a certain sense for production. Essentialty is defined to be a property such that without the good resource there will be no production of the consumption good under consideration at all. Later we will refine this definition.
Secondly we need to note that an initially essential resource will lose this quality with time by developping technologies to produce substitutive goods or to produce the consumption good without use of the resource. In other words: Production of the consumption good need not necessarily stop with ultimate exhaustion of the resource.
The effects of substitutive goods can be described by the elasticity of substitution between the resource and its substitute. Development of those substitutes will be enforced the higher the price of an essential exhaustible resource will increase due to the shortage of the resource.

II.1 Optimal Extraction Rates and Uncertainty with Respect to R&D towards Future Technologies

II.1.1 Exogeneous Technical Progress

The following analysis, based on P. Dasgupta and G. Heal (1974), considers the problem of uncertainty with respect to future production technologies. Since the development of such a technology will be influenced by the interest of the users of the exhaustible resource, we will look at the problem of optimal depletion of an exhaustible resource from the view of the consumers of that resource. I.e. we analyze which quantity of the resource should be used up in production in order to maximize its utility over a certain time horizon. The optimal flow of the resource will then be dependent on the size of the total stock of the resource and on the costs due to research and development for a new technology, which makes the use of the resource redundant and thus the resource inessential.

II.1.1.1 Basic Model

For illustration we first introduce a simple model of the well-known problem of "how to eat a cake of fixed size". Suppose, there is an economy, which has a fixed stock x^0 of a homogeneous good and a substitute of this commodity is already available and flows into production at a constant rate M. Further let C(t) denote the consumption rate of the economy at time t, and let U(C(t)) denote the benefit, generated by C(t). This utility function $U(\cdot)$ is supposed to be monotonically increasing, strictly concave, and twice differentiable.
Moreover we assumme that

$$\lim_{C \to 0} U'(C) = \infty, \text{ and let } \eta(C) = -C\frac{U''(C)}{U'(C)}$$

denote the elasticity of marginal utility with

$$\infty > \lim_{C \to 0} \eta(C) =: \eta > 0.$$

Then we have the optimization problem

$$\int_0^{\infty} e^{-rt} U(C(t))dt \quad \to \quad \max \tag{1}$$

subject to

$$\begin{aligned} &\dot{x}(t) = M - x(t) \\ &C(t) \geq 0, \ x(t) \geq 0, \ M \geq 0, \text{ and } x(0) = x^0. \end{aligned} \tag{2}$$

The Hamiltonian is

$$H = e^{-rt}U(C(t)) + \lambda(t)e^{-rt}(M-x(t)) + \mu(t)e^{-rt}x(t) \ , \tag{3}$$

where

$$\mu(t) \geq 0 \text{ and } \mu(t)x(t) = 0.$$

The multiplier of the constraint $C(t) \geq 0$ is neglected, since it is identical to zero. Then we have the well-known necessary optimality conditions

$$\lambda(t) = U'(C(t)) \tag{4}$$

and

$$\dot{\lambda}(t) = -\mu(t) + r\lambda(t). \tag{5}$$

By these two conditions the optimal consumption path is given by

$$\frac{\dot{C}}{C} = \frac{-r}{\eta(C)} + \frac{\mu(t)}{\eta(C)U'(C)} < 0. \tag{6}$$

Hence we have two periods, which possibly can repeat one another:

<u>Period 1 (x(t)>0):</u> Here we have

$$\frac{\dot{C}}{C} = \frac{-r}{\eta(C)} < 0. \tag{6'}$$

<u>Period 2 (x(t)=0):</u> Equation (6) applies in general.
We analyze only the case $M > 0$. Then period 1 holds until a certain time T is reached, and x^0 as well as T can be determined by the equations

$$\int_0^T C(t)dt = x^0 + MT$$

and

$$\lim_{t \to T-} C(t) = C_T = M \ . \tag{7}$$

Condition (7) we need for the extension of the model.
For $t>T$ period 2 holds and we have $C(t) = M$. Hence we set $\mu(t)=0$ for $0\leq t<T$ and

$$\mu(t) = \frac{r}{U'(M)} \quad \text{for } t \geq T.$$

Thus the Hamiltonian is concave and along the corresponding policy we have

$$\lim_{t\to\infty} e^{-rt}\lambda(t)x(t) = 0.$$

In summary we have the

Proposition (Dasgupta and Heal, 1974):

There exists a unique optimal policy for the optimization problem (1). If $M > 0$ holds, then this optimal policy consits exactly of period 1 up to time T, from when on $x(t) = 0$ holds, and of period 2 from time T on, and during this period $C(t) = M$ holds. If $M = 0$ holds, then the optimal policy consists only of period 1 and C^0 is chosen such that

$$\lim_{t\to\infty} x(t) = 0 .$$

II.1.1.2 First Extension: Production

Now we introduce the production sector into the economy considered. Suppose, there is a consumption good, which can be reproduced jointly with another commodity (e.g. energy). The quantity of the additional commodity is given, cannot be enlarged, and generates a benefit at the constant rate L.
The stock of the reproducible composite commodity is denoted by $K(t)$, and $Z(t)$ denotes the rate of service, provided by the second commodity at time t. Then efficient output is given by the production function $G(K(t),Z(t))$. G is assumed to be monotonically increasing, strictly concave, and twice differentiable with

$$G(0,Z) > 0,$$

$$\lim_{K\to\infty} \frac{\partial G}{\partial K}(K,L) < r,$$

and

$$\lim_{K\to 0} \frac{\partial G}{\partial K}(K,L) > r.$$

Then consumption possibilities can be predicted by the equation

$$\dot{K} = G(K(t),Z(t)) - C(t). \tag{8}$$

Now we search for time patterns $C^*(t)$ and $Z^*(t)$ maximizing (1) subject to

$$C(t)\geq 0,\ Z(t)\geq 0,\ K(t)\geq 0, \tag{2)'$$
equation (8), and $K^0 > 0$ given.

If we write $g(K) = G(K,L)$ and define $\bar{K}$ as the solution of $g'(\bar{K}) = r$, we have the following

Proposition (Dasgupta and Heal, 1974):

There exists a unique solution of the optimization problem (1). Along this optimal policy $Z(t) = L$ holds for all $t \geq 0$, and the economy tends in the long run to the stationary consumption rate $C=g(\bar{K})$.
If $K^0<\bar{K}$ holds, then along the optimal policy we have $\dot{C}(t)>0$ and $\dot{K}(t)>0$.

II.1.1.3 Second Extension: Exhaustible Resources

Now we introduce exhaustible resources such that the second commodity, necessary for production of the consumption good, is available only at a finite amount. I.e. we replace Z by the flow $q(t)$ of the exhaustible resource into production.
Then the production function is given by $F(K,q)$ and is assumed to be increasing, strictly concave, twice differentiable, linear homogeneous with elasticity of substitution σ, and

$$\lim_{q \to 0} F_q = \infty \ . \tag{9}$$

Here the consumption possibilities can be written as

$$\dot{K}(t) = F(K(t), q(t)) - C(t). \tag{8)'$$

Now we have the problem to determine paths $C^*(t)$ and $q^*(t)$, maximizing (1) subject to the constraints

$$C(t) \geq 0, \ K(t) \geq 0, \ q(t) \geq 0, \text{ equation (8)'}$$
$$K^0 = K(0) > 0 \quad \text{and} \tag{2)"}$$

$$\int_0^\infty q(t)dt \leq x^0 \ , \quad x^0 \geq 0 \ . \tag{10}$$

The Hamiltonian is

$$H = e^{-rt}U(C(t)) + e^{-rt}\lambda(t)(F(K,q)-C) - \mu q + e^{-rt}\nu(t)q, \tag{3)'$$

where

$$\nu(t) \geq 0 \text{ and } \nu(t)q(t) = 0$$

and

$$\mu \geq 0 \text{ and } \mu(x^0 - \int_0^\infty q(t)dt) = 0$$

hold.

Maximizing the Hamiltonian with respect to C, we derive the necessary condition

$$\lambda(t) = U'(C). \tag{4)'$$

Maximizing the Hamiltonian with respect to the extraction rate $q(t)$, we derive the necessary condition

$$\mu = e^{-rt}(\nu(t) + \lambda(t)\frac{\partial F}{\partial q}). \tag{5)'$$

Hence with constraints (2)", (10), and $q(t) > 0$ we have along an optimal policy

$$\mu = e^{-rt}\lambda(t)F_q.$$

Also by equation (9) we have the

Proposition (Dasgupta and Heal, 1974):

If there exists an optimal policy, then there exists a continuous extraction rate $q(t)$ with $q(t)>0$ for all $t>0$ or there exists a finite T with $q(t)>0$ for all $0\leq t<T$ and $q(t)=0$ for all $t\geq T$.

Hence we now have to discuss the existence problem of an optimal policy and whether the consumption rate necessarily declines along such a policy, if the resource is essential for production.
From now on the resource is called essential, if the elasticity of substitution σ is at most 1.
Then we have the following

Theorem (Dasgupta and Heal, 1974):

If σ $(0<\sigma<\infty)$ and $\eta>0$ are constant, and $r > \rho(1-\eta)$, where

$$\rho := \lim_{x\to\infty} \frac{f(x)}{x} \quad \text{with } f(x) := F(\frac{K}{q},1),$$

then there exists exactly one optimal policy.

II.1.1.4 Third Extension: Uncertainty about the Future Technological Development

Uncertainty about future technological development is related to the time T, when an essential resource becomes inessential by the development of a substitute.
Time T is therefore assumed to be a random variable with given probability distribution, respectively density.
Until time T is reached, we have the optimization problem (1) subject to the constraints (8)', (10), and (2)".
After time T another production technology follows, as described by the production function $G(K(t),Z(t))$, where $Z(t)$ denotes the service rate of the substitute. Further, M denotes the constant rate, at which the substitute and/or the resource flows into production after the technological innovation.

The constraints after time T are

$$\dot{K}(t) = G(K(t),Z(t))-C(t) \qquad (8)''$$

$$\dot{V}(t) = M - Z(t) \qquad (11)$$

$$Z(t)\geq 0,\ K(t)\geq 0,\ C(t)\geq 0,\ V(t)\geq 0 \text{ and} \qquad (12)$$

$$V(T) = x^0 - \int_0^T q(t)dt\ ,\ K(T) \text{ given.} \qquad (10)'$$

The meaning of V(t) is obvious. Time T is a random variable with density function $\omega(t)$, for which

$$\omega(t)>0 \text{ for } t>0\ ,\quad \int_0^\infty \omega(t)dt = 1\ ,\ \text{and } \Omega(t) := 1-\int_{-\infty}^{t}\omega(\tau)d\tau \qquad (13)$$

hold.

Now we have to maximize the expectation

$$E\left(\int_0^\infty e^{-rt}U(C(t))dt\right)\ .$$

In addition, the no-production case must be excluded. In other words: Along a feasible strategy the probability that the resource will be totally used up before the substitute will be available, has to equal zero.

Hence we set

$$W(K(t),V(t)) := \max \int_T^\infty e^{-rt(t-T)}U(C(t))dt$$

subject to the constraints (8)', (11), (12) und (10)'.

Then by (13) we have

$$E\left(\int_0^\infty e^{-rt}U(C(t))dt\right) =$$

$$= \int_0^\infty \omega(T)\left(\int_0^T e^{-rt}U(C(t))dt + W(K(T),V(T))e^{-rT}\right)dT =$$

$$= \int_0^\infty e^{-rt}\left(U(C(t))\Omega(t) + \omega(t)W(K(t),V(t))\right)dt\ .$$

Now we have to maximize this functional subject to (8)', (2)', and

$$\dot{x}(t) = -q(t), \tag{14}$$
$$V(t) = x(t). \tag{15}$$

It can be shown that this optimization problem is equivalent to the problem of maximizing

$$\int_0^\infty e^{-\rho t} U(C(t))dt$$

subject to (2)', (8)', (14), (15), and the condition that the discount factor ρ is independent upon the path, which the economy follows, and

$$W_K = W_x = 0 \quad \text{for all } K(t) \text{ and } x(t) , \tag{16}$$

$$\rho(t) = r(t) + \int_0^t \psi(\tau)d\tau, \text{ where } \psi(t) := \frac{\omega(t)}{\Omega(t)} . \tag{17}$$

$\psi(t)$ denotes the conditional probability that the substitute will be developped at time T under the condition that it will not be developped before T.
The model assumes that technical progress is costless, and the point in time, at which it will become effective, is randomly, i.e. exogenously given. However, the scarcity of an exhaustible resource and the development of a substitute do actually correspond. Thus we turn to a model (Kamien and Schwartz, 1977) of endogenous technical progress.

II.1.2 Endogenous Technical Progress

II.1.2.1 Basic Model

Differently to the assumptions of Dasgupta and Heal we now assume that the point in time, when a new technology will be available, is a random variable, yet can partially controlled by the intensity of research and development towards this new technology. More precisely, it will be assumed that the probability of advancing a new technology fundamentally ("breakthrough innovation") is an increasing function of cumulative research effort; in R&D a commodity is used, which can only

be produced by drawing on an exhaustible resource. The consumption good under consideration can be produced by the input of a reproducible factor (like e.g. capital) and by an exhaustible resource.
The output has to be distributed among the three sectors consumption, research, and/or expansion of the capital stock. The objective is to maximize discounted benefit given by consumption of the produced good. For the utility function and for the production function, the assumptions of II.1.1 apply.
Hence the production function F can be written as follows:

$$F(K,q) = Kf(y) \quad \text{with}$$

$$y := \frac{q}{K} \quad \text{and} \quad f(y) := F(1,\frac{q}{K}).$$

Further we have

$$f(0) = 0 \ , \ f' > 0 \ , \ \lim_{y\to 0} f'(y) = \infty \ , \ f'' < 0.$$

The remaining resource stock x(t) will be diminished according to

$$\begin{aligned} \dot{x}(t) &= -q(t) = -K(t)y(t) \\ x(0) &= x^0 > 0 \ , \ x(t) \geq 0. \end{aligned} \tag{18}$$

Neglecting research and development we would have the same problem as above, namely to determine non-negative time patterns for consumption C(t), productive capital K(t), the resource stock x(t), and resource extraction q(t) so as to maximize (1) subject to the constraints (18) and

$$\dot{K}(t) = K(t)f(y(t)) - C(t) \ , \ K(0) = K^0 > 0 \ , \ K(t) \geq 0. \qquad (8)'''$$

Condition (8)''' means that the output is used in part by consumption and by expansion of the capital stock.
From time T, the point of implementing a radically new technology, we have the benefit

$$W = \max \int_T^\infty e^{-r(t-T)} U(C(t))dt \ . \tag{19}$$

Until then one part of the consumption good flows into R&D towards the new technology with the rate m(t). Further let z(t) denote the cumulative effective research effort. The increase of z(t) is given by a bounded, concave, strictly monotonically increasing, and twice differentiable function g(m(t)):

$$\dot{z}(t) = g(m(t)) \quad , \quad z(0) = 0 \tag{20}$$
$$g(0) = 0 \quad , \quad 0 < g' < \infty \quad , \quad g'' < 0.$$

Furthermore, let $\Phi(z)$ denote the probability distribution function of the random variable, which gives the time of the breakthrough of the new technology. In other words: $\Phi(z)$ denotes the probability that the new technology will be developped at time $t{:}z(t)=z$. Φ is assumed to be twice differentiable with

$$\Phi(0) = 0 \ , \quad \Phi'(0) = 0 \ , \quad \Phi' > 0 \quad \text{and} \quad \lim_{z\to\infty} \Phi(z) = 1 \tag{21}$$

Since time T, when the exhaustible resource will be no longer essential because of successful research, is unknown, the optimization problem has to be partitioned into two periods: The objective function for the second period is given by equation (19).
During the first period, when the old technology is still in use, the benefit U(C(t)) is given at time t with probability $1-\Phi(z(t))$.
The new technology will become available during the time interval (t,t+dt) with probability

$$\frac{d\Phi(z(t))}{dt} = \Phi'(z(t))\dot{z}(t) = \Phi'(z(t))g(m(t)) \ .$$

In summary we have to maximize the functional

$$\int_0^\infty e^{-rt}(U(C)(1-\Phi(z)) + \Phi'(z)g(m)W)dt \tag{22}$$

with respect to the consumption rate C(t), research effort m(t), and the factor ratio y(t), subject to (20) and

$$\dot{K} = Kf(y) - C - m \qquad K(0) = K^0 \ , \quad K(t) > 0 \ ; \tag{23}$$

$$\dot{x} = -Ky \ , \quad x(0) = x^0 \ , \quad x(t) > 0; \tag{24}$$

The Hamiltonian is

$$H = U(C)(1-\Phi(z))+\Phi'(z)g(m)W+\lambda(Kf(y)-C-m)-\mu Ky+\nu g(m). \tag{25}$$

From (25) one derives the necessary conditions for maximizing paths C, m, y, K, x, z:

$$\frac{\partial H}{\partial C} = U'(C)(1-\Phi(z)) - \lambda = 0 \tag{26}$$

$$\frac{\partial H}{\partial m} = \Phi'(z)g'(m)W - \lambda + \nu g'(m) \leq 0 \tag{27}$$

$$\frac{\partial H}{\partial y} = \lambda Kf'(y) - \mu K = 0 \tag{28}$$

By the assumptions that marginal utility for $C \to 0$ as well as marginal productivity of the exhaustible resource tend to infinity for $q \to 0$, we can simplify (26) and (28) as follows:

$$U'(C)(1-\Phi(z)) = \lambda \quad \text{and} \tag{26'}$$

$$\lambda f'(y) = \mu, \tag{28'}$$

while (27) can be written

$$\left.\begin{array}{ll} (\Phi'(z)W+\nu)g'(m) = \lambda & \text{if } m > 0, \\ (\Phi'(z)W+\nu)g'(0) \leq 0 & \text{if } m = 0 \end{array}\right. \tag{27'}$$

The multipliers λ, μ, and ν can be interpreted as follows: λ is the marginal value of the capital stock, μ the marginal value of the available reserves, and ν the marginal value of cumulative effective research effort. By the transversality conditions for a finite time horizon one derives

$$\nu(t) = -\Phi'(z)W + \int_t^\infty e^{-r(s-t)}\Phi'(z(s))(rW-U(C(s)))ds.$$

Now we can rewrite (27)

$$g'(m)\int_t^\infty e^{-r(s-t)}\Phi'(z(s))(rW-U(C(s)))ds \leq \lambda, \tag{27''}$$

where equality applies, if $m > 0$.

I.e., if the consumption good is used for R&D, its marginal value equals the marginal value of using it for expansion of the capital stock.
Furthermore, we have

$$\nu(0) = \int_0^\infty e^{-rs}\Phi'(z(s))(rW-U(C(s)))ds \ ;$$

Hence $\nu(0)=0$, if no research takes place, since then $\Phi' \equiv 0$ applies, and $\nu(0) > 0$ holds, if expected benefit, given by innovation, is positive.
To determine the dynamics of y, we get by rearrangement of (28) the following differential equation, depending only on production:

$$y' = f'(f-yf')/f'' < 0.$$

The ratio of the input of the exhaustible resource and of capital hence decreases over time.
Similarly one derives the dynamics of consumption

$$\frac{U''C'}{-U'} = f(y) - yf'(y) - r - g(m)h(z) \qquad (29)$$

with

$$h(z) := \frac{\Phi'(z)}{1-\Phi(z)} \ .$$

The consumption rate increases or decreases depending on whether the right hand side of (29) is positive or negative.
To determine the optimal research effort we rewrite equation (27) as follows:

$$s(t) := (\Phi'(z)W+\nu)g'(m) - \lambda \leq 0. \qquad (27)'''$$

Since $z(0)=0$ and $\Phi'(0)=0$ one can choose $s(t)$ and m at initial time 0 such that either

$$m(0) = 0 \quad \text{and} \quad s(0) = \nu(0)g'(0)-\lambda(0) < 0$$

or

$$s(0) = \nu(0)g'(m(0))-\lambda(0) = 0.$$

Suppose, there exists a period $0 \leq t \leq t_0$, when $m(t)=0$ holds, then, because of $m=z=0$ during this period and because of $\Phi'(0)=g(0)=0$, one derives

$$\nu(t) = e^{rt}\nu(0)$$

and

$$s(t) = e^{rt}(\nu(0)g'(0) - \frac{\mu(0)}{f'(y)}) < 0$$

where

$$\mu(t) = e^{rt}\mu(0).$$

Since the expression $\nu(0)g'(0)-(\mu(0)/f'(y))$ increases with time, there exists a $t_0<\infty$ with $s(t_0)=0$ and R&D towards a new technology starts.

Up to this time t_0, which can be initial time 0, the economy is described by the model of II.1.1.3.

Hence we only have to analyze the following period, when research takes place, i.e. for $m(t)>0$.

Differentiating the first part of (27)' with respect to time, one derives

$$(\varphi''\dot{z}W+\dot{\nu})g' + (\varphi\dot{W}+\dot{\nu})g''\dot{m} = \dot{\lambda}$$

and hence jointly with the corresponding optimality condition (26)-(28),

$$-\lambda g''\frac{\dot{m}}{g'} = \lambda(f-yf') - (rW-U)\varphi'g'.$$

and finally

$$-\frac{g''\dot{m}}{g'} = f(y) - yf'(y) - (rW-U(C))\frac{g'(m)h(z)}{U'(C)}.$$

By property (20) of g, the rate of research increases, whenever the right hand side is positive, and it decreases, if the right hand side is negative.

If all three control variables are positive, one derives the following statements on C:

a) If $h(z) = 0$, then

$$\text{sgn}(\dot{C}) = \text{sgn}(f-yf'-r)$$

b) If $f-yf' \leq r$ at time s, then $\dot{C}(t) < 0$ holds for all $t > s$.

c) If $h(z)>0$ and $f-yf' > r$, then

$$\left.\begin{array}{l}\dot{C}(t)<0\\ \dot{C}(t)>0\end{array}\right\} \quad \text{if} \quad \left\{\begin{array}{l}m(t)<m^U(t)\\ m(t)>m^U(t),\end{array}\right.$$

where $m^U(t)$ is defined implicitly by

$$g(m^U(t)) = (f-yf'-r)/h(z)|_t \ .$$

About $\dot{m}$ one derives the following statements:

a) If $h(z)=0$, then $\dot{m}(t)\geq 0$, where equality holds, if and only, if $m(t)=0$ holds.

b) If $(f-yf')/h(z)g'(0)|_t > G(C^*)$, then $\dot{m}(t)<0$ holds, where $G(C) := (rW-U(C))/U'(C)$ and C^* denotes the value of C, which maximizes G.

c) If $(f-yf')/h(z)g'(0)|_t < G(C^*)$, then

$$\left.\begin{array}{l}\dot{m}(t)<0\\ \dot{m}(t)>0\end{array}\right\} \quad \text{if} \quad \left\{\begin{array}{l}m(t)<m^C(C(t),t)\\ m(t)>m^C(C(t),t).\end{array}\right.$$

Here $m^C(C,t)$ is defined implicitly by $m^C(C,t)=m$ in the equation

$$(f-yf')/h(z)g'(m) = (rW-U(C))/U'(C).$$

After having analyzed consumption C and research effort m separately we now combine both paths in order to obtain an optimal policy.

1. $f-yf'|_{t_m} < r$:

From time t_m on we have $\dot{C}(t)<0$ and $\dot{m}(t_m)>0$. When time passes, possibly case c) for the path of m applies so that from a certain time t* on $\dot{m} < 0$ holds:

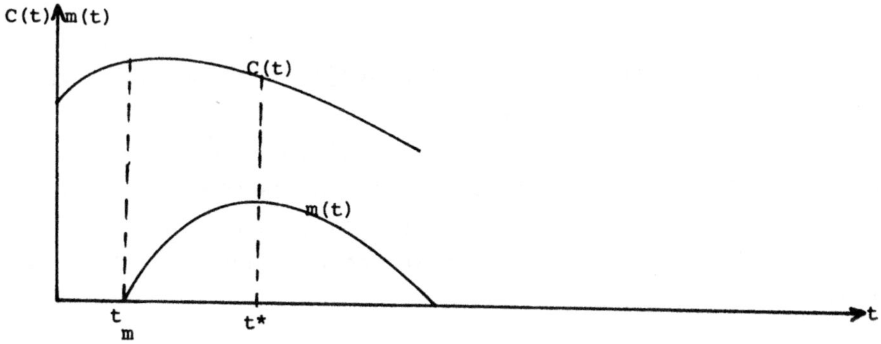

2. $f - yf'|_{t_m} > r$:

We have $C(t_m) > 0$ and $m(t_m) > 0$ and the time profiles are given either one of the two following figures:

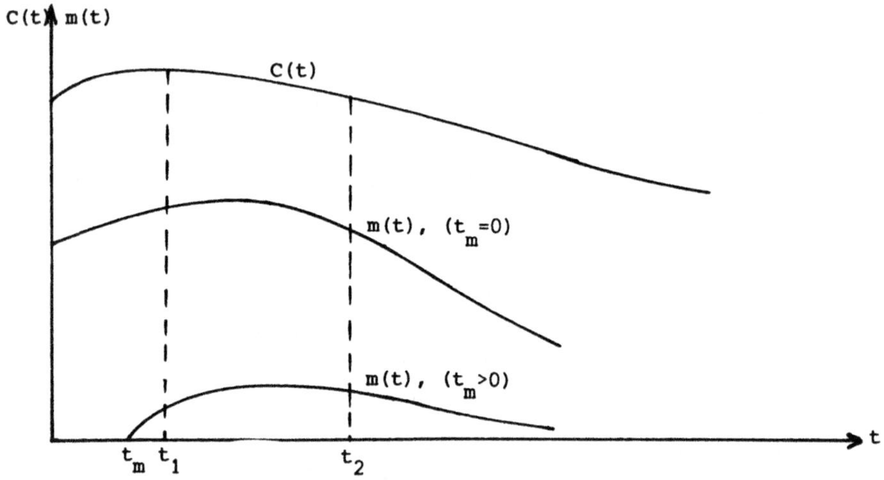

2'.

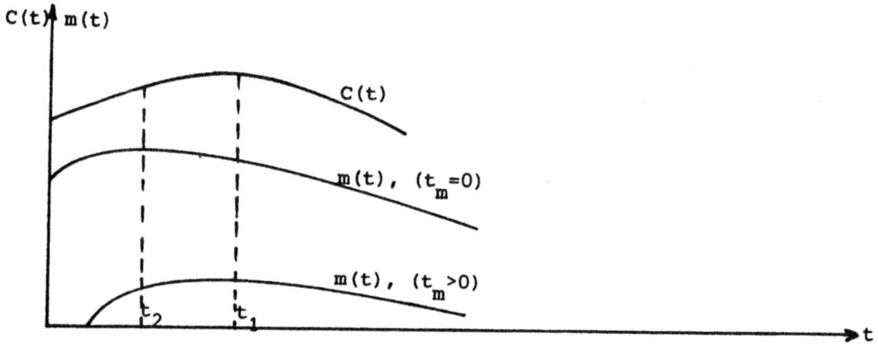

These patterns can be obtained in projecting the paths C(t) and m(t) into C-m-phase space.

The difference between 2. and 2'. is given by the $\dot{C} = 0$ locus crossing the optimal path at time t_1 and by the $\dot{m} = 0$ locus crossing the optimal path at time $t_2 > t_1$ in case 2.

In case 2'. the optimal path first crosses the $\dot{m} = 0$ locus and after this crosses the $\dot{C} = 0$ locus.

II.1.2.2 Modification of the Basic Model

Technical progress will now be understood that the economy tries to develop a production technology by capital input, independent on the input of an exhaustible resource.
Now $z(t)$ denotes the state of knowledge about a new technology and K_D denotes cumulative capital for the development of the technology.
The dynamics of knowledge are then given by

$$z(t) = f(K_D) \quad , \quad z(0) = z^0. \tag{30}$$

The total capital stock is composed of two classes of capital:

$$K = K_P + K_D, \tag{31}$$

where K_P denotes the capital for production.
Suppose, the new technology will be available, when a certain level of knowledge, say Z, will be reached. Z is random, and T denotes the point of time, at which $z = Z$; i.e. time T, at which the new technology breakthrough occurs, is a function of the random variable Z.
For the probability density function ω of Z see (13).
After time T the economy is governed by other state equations and hence we have the optimization problem

$$W(K) := \max(e^{rt}\int_T^{\infty} e^{-rt}U(C)dt)$$

subject to the corresponding new constraints for the time after T.
I.e. the optimization problem corresponds to the model of Dasgupta and Heal (1974) (see (1)', (2)', (8)', (14)-(17)) for the time after technical breakthrough. As the new technology is independent on the input of the exhaustible resource, the function $W = W(K)$ depends only on capital input.
Summarizing we have to maximize the expected value

$$E(\int_0^{\infty} e^{-rt}U(C)dt)$$

with

$$E(\int_0^\infty e^{-rt}U(C)dt) =$$

$$E(\int_0^T e^{-rt}U(C)dt + \int_T^\infty e^{-rt}U(C)dt) =$$

$$E(\int_0^T e^{-rt}U(C)dt + e^{-rt}W(K)) =$$

$$\int_{Z_0}^\infty w(Z)\lfloor \int_0^T e^{-rt}U(C)dt + e^{-rt}W(K)\rfloor dZ \tag{32}$$

subject to (30) and

$$\dot{x}(t) = -q(t) \quad , \quad x(0) = x^0 \tag{33}$$

$$\dot{K}(t) = Y(K_P,q) - C = Y(K-K_D,q) - C . \tag{8)''''$$

With

$$\Omega(z) := \int_z^\infty \omega(s)ds , \tag{13)'$$

the probability of breakthrough of the new technology after reaching the level of knowledge z, (32) equals

$$\int_0^\infty e^{-rt}\lfloor U(C)\Omega(z)+\omega(z)Wf(K_D)\rfloor dt. \tag{32)'$$

The state variables of the control problem above are z, K, and x, and the control variables are K_D, C, and q.
The Hamiltonian of this problem is

$$H = e^{-rt}[(U\Omega+\omega Wf) + \lambda f + \mu(Y-C) - \nu q + \xi f], \tag{34}$$

where λ, μ and ν are the present values of the prices of z, K, and x, respectively; ξ denotes the multiplier with respect to the constraint $f(K_D) > 0$, such that along an optimal path

$$e^{-rt}\xi f = 0 \tag{35}$$

holds.

The dynamics of optimal consumption can be derived from the necessary optimality conditions and are given by

$$\frac{\dot{C}}{C} = - \frac{r < \psi f - \frac{d}{dt}(\log(Y_q))}{\eta} , \tag{36}$$

where $\psi := \omega/\Omega$ and $\eta := -CU''/U'$ hold, and ψ can be interpreted as the conditional probability of the new technology being available at time $T = t(z)$, subject to the condition of not having been available before T; η denotes the elasticity of marginal utility.

By (36) and by the necessary conditions due to the Hamiltonian (34) we finally derive the following three equations, characterizing an optimal policy:

$$\frac{d}{dt}(\log Y_q) = Y_K + \frac{W_K \psi f}{U'}, \tag{37}$$

$$C(t) = C(0)\left(\frac{e^{-rt}\Omega Y_q}{Y_q(0)}\right)^{1/\eta}, \tag{38}$$

$$Y_{K_D} \frac{d}{dt}\left(\log \frac{Y_q f_{K_D}}{Y_{K_D}}\right) = f_{K_D} \psi \frac{U - rW + \dot{W}}{U'}. \tag{39}$$

II.1.2.3 Example with Exponentially Distributed Z

For illustration of the above solutions let us assume that Y is a Cobb-Douglas production function,

$$Y = K_P^{\alpha} q^{1-\alpha} , \quad 0 < \alpha < 1 , \tag{40}$$

the function, describing the research effort, is linear,

$$f(K_D) = \beta K_D \tag{41}$$

and the random variable Z is shifted exponentially distributed,

$$\omega(z) = \gamma e^{-\gamma(z-z_0)} . \tag{42}$$

Due to the special property of the exponential distribution of having "no memory" we have $\psi = \gamma$.
Even though this assumption strictly makes less sense within our context, we will discuss this specialization for illustration and ease of formal exposition.
Further we assume that the technical breakthrough will take place such that it is possible to get certain utility U^0 immediately.
With this assumption we have $W = (1/r)U^0$
With $v(t):=Kp/q$ (37) - (39) yield

$$v^{1-\alpha} = (1-\alpha)(t+B), \tag{37)'$$

$$C(t) = (\eta-1)\frac{\alpha}{\beta\gamma(1-\alpha)^2(t+B)^2} =: C_1(t) \tag{38)'$$

and

$$z(t) = z^0 - \frac{rt}{\gamma} < \frac{1}{\gamma}(\frac{\alpha}{1-\alpha}+2\eta)\log\frac{t+B}{B}, \tag{39)'$$

where B is a positive constant.
By (39)' one can obtain that there exists a point of time, t_f, with $z(t_f) = 0$. Since z can be interpreted as the state of knowledge, z cannot decrease. However, this is assured by (35). Hence t_f can be interpreted as the time, when capital will no longer be put into the development of a new technology and the state of knowledge remains constant. Therefore the three equations (37)' - (39)' are only valid either during the period, until t_f will be reached or until the new technology breakthrough occurs, if this happens before t_f.
On capital input into research and development one derives from (30) and (41)

$$K_D(t) = \frac{-r}{\beta\gamma} + \frac{\alpha/(1-\alpha)+2\eta}{\beta\gamma(t+B)} \tag{43}$$

Hence one can derive t_f, from when on $K_D \equiv 0$ holds.
Capital input into production, K_P, can be derived by (40), (8)"", and (38)':

$$Kp(t) = Kp(0)(\frac{t+B}{B})^{1/(1-\alpha)} + \frac{G(1-\alpha)}{\beta\gamma(2-\alpha)}(t+B)^{1/(1-\alpha)} \cdot \tag{44}$$

$$\cdot\ (B^{(\alpha-2)/(1-\alpha)}-(t+B)^{(\alpha-2)/(1-\alpha)}),$$

where

$$G = -\left(\frac{(\eta-1)\alpha}{(1-\alpha)^2} - \frac{\alpha}{1-\alpha} - 2\eta\right).$$

K_p is strictly monotonically increasing and strictly convex.
With

$$P := (1-\alpha)^{-1/(1-\alpha)}\ , \quad Q := A^{-1/(1-\alpha)}\ , \quad \text{and}$$

$$R := \frac{G(1-\alpha)}{\beta\gamma(2-\alpha)}$$

one derives the optimal extraction rate

$$q^*(t) = P(K_p(0)Q + RB^{(\alpha-2)/1-\alpha)}(t+B)^{1/(1-\alpha)}$$

$$-(t+B)^{(\alpha-2)/(1-\alpha)}R(t+B)^{1/(1-\alpha)})$$

and finally the resource stock, available at time t

$$x^*(t) = x^0 - Ht + J(Q - (t+B)^{-1/(1-\alpha)}),$$

where

$$H = P(K_p(0)Q + RA^{(\alpha-2)/(1-\alpha)})$$

and

$$J = R^{(1-2\alpha)/(1-\alpha)}\ .$$

The graphs of those two functions are given by the following figure:

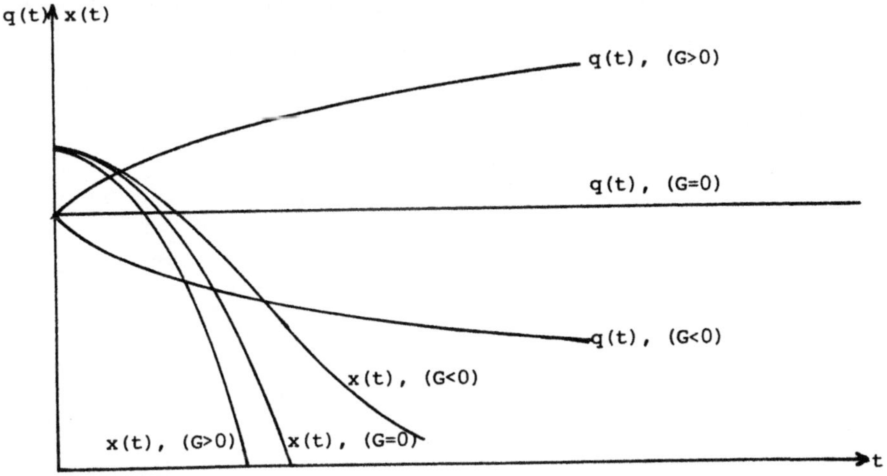

Due to $\mathrm{sgn}(G) = -\mathrm{sgn}(C+\dot{K}_D) = -\mathrm{sgn}(Y-\dot{K}_P)$ (see (38)′ and (43)) only the case $G < 0$ can occur, since only then production Y can be greater than capital input K_P. I.e. the resource does not need to be totally exhausted.

The specialized model shows the somewhat surprising result that there will be no longer capital input into research and development towards a production technology, independent on resource input, from a certain time t_f on, and this point of time is independent from the remaining amount of the resource. Obviously this situation empirically is rather unlikely, since the readiness to invest into research and development is just conditioned by the scarcity of the resource, and should consequently rise with the shortage of the resource. This could be explicable at best, if initially the scarcity of the resource seemed to be so threatening that an alternative is searched for. However, with time it turns out that the exhaustible resource will be always available. Actually, if production continues, this can only occur, if the resource is not exhaustible.

The model totally neglects the demand of the consumption good, produced in using the resource, or, respectively, it is implicitly assumed that there is always demand for the commodity. However, this demand could be satisfied only by other production technologies due to the scarceness of the resource. This, however, is a contradiction to the result that there will be no investment for a new technology, before the state of knowledge, necessary for its realization, is reached.

This dilemma is given by the assumption of Z being exponentially distributed. For precisely by this assumption the development of an alternative technology is independent on the remaining amount of the resource. Time t_f, when the program of innovation will break off, depends on the discount rate r. The smaller r, the later t_f will be. Strictly the example can at best illustrate, how the model can be applied formally.

II.2 Optimal Extraction Rates and Unknown Reserves

Until now we discussed models of uncertainty with respect to research and development for a substitute production technology. The research effort, respectively the time of breakthrough of a new technology was assumed to be random.
The subsequent model (see Pan-Tai Liu, 1980) analyzes randomness with respect to the resource stock size. The only knowledge about the amount available is given by a probability distribution function. For ease of exposition it is assumed that the exploitation of the resource stock is controlled by exactly one decision maker, i.e. a monopolist. The state equation regarding resource extraction is given by

$$\frac{dx}{dt} = q(t) \ , \quad x(0) = 0 \ , \quad 0 \leq x \leq x_m \ , \quad q \geq 0. \tag{45}$$

Here x(t) denotes the cumulative quantity of the resource, extracted up to time t, and q(t) denotes, as above, the extraction rate.
The initial amount Z of the resource is assumed to be a continuously distributed random variable with probability distribution function $1-F(x)$, $0 \leq x \leq x_m$, i.e.

$$F(x) = P(Z>x) \text{ with } F(0) = 1, \ F(x_m) = 0 \ , \ F'(x) < 0, \text{ and}$$

F is continuously differentiable.
This means that x_m denotes the biggest size of the resource stock possible.
The decision maker determines an extraction policy in order to maximize the expected discounted utility

$$J = E(\int_0^\infty e^{-rt} U(\Pi(t))dt) \quad \rightarrow \quad \max \ , \tag{46}$$

where U denotes a utility function and

$$\Pi(t) := p(q(t))-c(x,q) \tag{47}$$

denotes the monopolist's profit at time t.
Utility U is assumed to satisfy the usual conditions:

$$U(0)=0, \ U'(\Pi)>0, \ U''(\Pi)<0 \text{ for all } \Pi<0, \text{ and}$$
$$\lim_{\Pi \to 0} U'(\Pi) = \infty \tag{48}$$

Assuming $E(\tau(\omega))<\infty$, where $\tau(\omega)$ denotes the (random) time, when $x(t)=Z$ holds, and ω denotes the probability measure of the basic probability space, then (46) is equivalent to

$$J = \int_0^\infty e^{-rt}U(\Pi(t))F(x(t))dt. \tag{46'}$$

II.2.1 Monopolistic Extraction Rates Depending on Time only

Applying the maximum principle one derives the optimal extraction rate

$$q^*(t) = \begin{cases} q^*(x^*,\Phi), & x^* \in S \\ 0, & x^* \in \bar{S}, \end{cases} \tag{49}$$

where S denotes the admissible region $\{x|0\leq x<x_m \text{ and } p'(0)-c_q(x,0)>0\}$ and Φ the solution of the following differential equation:

$$\dot{\Phi} = r\Phi - U(\Pi^*)F'(x^*) + U(\Pi^*)c_x(x^*,q^*)F(x^*) . \tag{50}$$

Inserting (49) into the state equation (45) and into equation (50) one obtains a system of differential equations for x^* and Φ, the solution of which depends on the following assumptions on the asymptotic behaviour of x^* and Φ:

(i) $\lim_{t\to\infty} \Phi(t) = 0$, if $\lim_{t\to\infty} x^*(t) = \hat{x} < x_m$

or

(ii) $\lim_{t\to\infty} \Phi(t) = \alpha < 0$, if $\lim_{t\to\infty} x^*(t) = x_m$.

<u>Case (i):</u> $S = [0,\hat{x})$ and $x^* \in S$ for all $t > 0$:

The system of the two differential equations can be solved in the subsequent way:

1. Choose "initial solutions" of x^* and Φ, say $x^*=x-\varepsilon_1$ and $\Phi=\varepsilon_2$, where ε_i (i=1,2) denote arbitrarily small positive numbers.
2. Integrate the state equation (45) and equation (50) backward; the solutions may be $x^*=x^*(t,\varepsilon_1,\varepsilon_2)$ and $\Phi=\Phi(t,\varepsilon_1,\varepsilon_2)$.

3. Compute the limits

$$x^*(t) = \lim_{\varepsilon_1 \to 0, \varepsilon_2 \to 0} x^*(t, \varepsilon_1, \varepsilon_2) \text{ and}$$

$$\Phi(t) = \lim_{\varepsilon_1 \to 0, \varepsilon_2 \to 0} \Phi(t, \varepsilon_1, \varepsilon_2).$$

Case (ii): $S = [0, x_m)$ and $x^*(t) \in S$ for all $t \geq 0$:
Setting $\Phi=0$ in equation (50) one derives

$$\alpha = (1/r) \lim_{x \to x_m, q \to 0} [U(\Pi)F'(x) - U'(\Pi)c_x(x,q)F(x)]$$

and the differential equations can be solved as in case (i) with "initial solutions" $x_m - \varepsilon_1$ and $\alpha - \varepsilon_2$ for x^* and Φ, respectively.
After having determined x^* and Φ, one can finally determine the optimal depletion rate $q^*(t)$.
For the problem of total exhaustion of the resource one derives the following results:
In case (i) we have

$$P(x^*(t) \geq Z \text{ for a certain } t>0) = 1 ,$$

i.e. the reserve will be totally depleted with probability 1.
In case (ii)

$$P(x^*(t) < Z \text{ for all } t \geq 0) = P(x<Z) = F(x) \leq 1$$

i.e. the resource will not be totally exhausted (in probability). This may be, either if the marginal revenue is not high enough for extraction, or if the extraction costs increase beyond profitability of extraction.

II.2.2 Monopolistic Extraction Rates Depending on Time and Quantities, already Extracted

Now optimal controls $q^*(x,t)$ will also take into account the quantities, already extracted.

First we analyze the corresponding static problem of maximizing $U(\Pi)$. The necessary condition for U to be a maximal point is given by

$$\frac{\partial U}{\partial q} = (p'(q) - c_q(x,q))U'(\Pi) = 0.$$

Due to the assumption $U' > 0$ this yields

$$p'(q) - c_q(x,q) = 0,$$

from which one derives the optimal $q = \bar{q}(x)$.

To solve the dynamic version of the problem, $x^*(t) \in S$ must hold for all $t \geq 0$.

Further, we have for each $x \in S$, especially for $x = x^*$, the value function

$$V(x,t) = \max \int_t^\infty e^{-rs} U(\Pi(s))F(x(s))ds.$$

By dynamic optimization one derives

$$V(x,t) = V(x)e^{-rt},$$

where $V(x)$ satisfies for each $x \in S$ the condition

$$\max_{q \geq 0} \lfloor V'(x)q - rV(x) + U(\Pi)F(x) \rfloor =: V'(x)q^* - rV(x) + U(\Pi^*)F(x) = 0 \ . \tag{51}$$

Differentiating (51) with respect to q, one obtains

$$V'(x) = -(p'(q^*) - c_q(x,q^*))U'(\Pi^*)F(x) \ . \tag{52}$$

Since $q^*(x) \geq 0$, it follows that $V'(x) \leq 0$ for all $x \in S$.

Hence

$$p'(q^*) - c_q(x,q^*) \geq 0$$

holds, since $U' > 0$ and $F > 0$.

This yields $q^*(x) \leq \bar{q}(x)$; i.e. the optimal extraction rate in the dynamic case cannot exceed that one in the static case. This is obviously plausible, since in the dynamic version of the model future demand has to be considered.
Inserting (52) into the right-hand side of (51), one observes

$$V(x) = (1/r)\lfloor U(\Pi^*)-(p'(q^*)-c_q(x,q^*)q^*U'(\Pi^*)\rfloor F(x).$$

By the mean value theorem it follows that $V > 0$ for all $x \in S$.
Differentiating V with respect to x, inserting V' into equation (52), and rearranging one derives the following first order differential equation for q^*

$$\lfloor U'(\Pi^*)(p''(q^*)-c_{qq}(x,q^*))-U''(\Pi^*)(p'(q^*)-c_q(x,q^*))\rfloor q^*q^{*\prime} =$$

$$= \lfloor U'(\Pi^*)(p'(q^*)-c_q(x,q^*))q^*-U(\Pi^*\rfloor(F'(x)/F(x) +$$

$$+ \lfloor c_{qx}(x,q^*)q^*-c_x(x,q^*)\rfloor U'(\Pi^*) -$$

$$- \lfloor rU'(\Pi^*)+U''(\Pi^*)c_x(x,q^*)q^*\rfloor\lfloor p'(q^*)-c_q(x,q^*)\rfloor$$

for all $x \in S$.

If there exists a unique solution q^* of this differential equation, for which $0 < q^*(x) \leq q(x)$ and
either

$$\lim_{x\to\hat{x}} q^*(x) = 0\ , \quad \text{if } S = \lfloor 0,\hat{x})$$

or

$$\lim_{x\to x_m} q^*(x) = 0\ , \quad \text{if } S = \lfloor 0,x_m) \quad \text{hold,}$$

then q^* is an optimal control.
This differential equation shows that in case of uncertainty the resource will be exploited slower than in the case that the size of the resource stock would be known. This fact can be interpreted in the way that the decision maker will exploit his resource stock more cautiously, since he has to anticipate premature total exhaustion of the stock.

II.2.3 Optimal Extraction Rates and Pure Competition

II.2.3.1 Basic Model

Now we assume that n suppliers exploit a common stock of the resource, the size of which is only known by a probability distribution function. The solution of the corresponding optimization problem will be a Pareto optimum. Analogous to the preceding model we have the state equations

$$\dot{x}_i = q_i \qquad x_i(0) = x_i^0 \qquad (i=1,2,\ldots,n) \tag{45}'$$

where $q_i > 0$ and $0 < \sum_{i=1}^{n} x_i = X < X_m$ hold.

Once again Z denotes a random variable with probability distribution function

$$F(X)=P(Z>X) \text{ with } F(0)=1 , \quad F(X_m)=0, \text{and } F'(X)<0.$$

Each firm's objective is to maximize

$$J_i = \int_0^\infty e^{-rt} U_i(\Pi_i)F(X)dt \qquad (i=1,2,\ldots,n). \tag{46}''$$

A Pareto optimal allocation of the resource is given, if there exist real numbers $\gamma_i > 0$ such that the functional

$$J = \sum_{i=1}^{n} \gamma_i J_i$$

is maximal with respect to the optimal controls q_i^*.
Due to the formal difficulty of this problem we restrict our discussion to the following example.

II.2.3.2 Example with two Suppliers

Suppose, the utility functions are given by $U_i = \Pi_i^\alpha$ with $0 < \alpha < 1$, here $\alpha=1/2$, $p_1=2q_1$, $p_2=q_2$, $\gamma_1=\gamma_2$, $c_i=Xq_i$ and $X_m=1$.
By the corresponding system of differential equations (see II.2.1), which can be derived just as in case of one decision maker, one

obtains the following trajectory in the phase space:

$$\frac{dx_1}{dx_2} = \frac{2-X}{1-X} = \frac{2-x_1-x_2}{1-x_1-x_2} \; .$$

The solution of this differential equation is given by

$$3 - 2(x_1+x_2) = Ae^{2(x_2-x_1)}, \quad \text{A constant.}$$

This represents a bundle of curves lying inside the triangle

$\{(x_1,x_2) | x_1 > 0,\; x_2 > 0,\; x_1+x_2 < 1\}$

and ending on the hypotenuse.

II.2.4 Optimal Extraction Rates from Consumer's View

II.2.4.1 Basic Model

Another analysis of the problem of randomness of the resource stock size was elaborated by G. C. Loury (1978): Once again let Z denote a random variable, which gives the unknown total yet finite amount of the resource, for which a probability distribution function of Z is known. I.e. we have at each point of time information on the reserves of the resource by the distribution of Z subject to the condition of the amount of the resource, already exploited.

Further it is assumed that at each instant of time supply and demand of the resource are equal, i.e. the market structure of the supplying side is postulated away.

The corresponding optimization problem is given as follows:

Maximize

$$J = E(\int_0^T e^{-rt} U(C(t))dt) \tag{46'''}$$

with given probability distribution function F and subject to the constraints

$$\int_0^T C(t)dt \leq Z \quad \text{and } C(t) \geq 0 \quad \text{for all } 0 \leq t \leq T \; . \tag{53}$$

The expected amount of the reserves is assumed to be of finite size:

$$\int_0^\infty x dF(x) < \infty . \tag{54}$$

For the utility function U assumptions (48) apply.
Furthermore, the expectation of the objective function is related to the random time horizon T, due to condition (53). Let $G_C(T)$ denote the continuous probability distribution function, which gives the probability that the resource will be exhausted, if the extraction path C(t) is followed up, i.e.

$$G_C(T) = P(Z< \int_0^T C(t)dt) = F(\int_0^T C(t)dt) =: F(X_T).$$

Then we can rewrite the optimization problem above as follows:
Maximize

$$J = \int_0^\infty \int_0^T e^{-rt} U(C(t))f(X_T)C(T)dtdT \qquad (46)''''$$

subject to the single constraint $C(t) > 0$.
For optimal extraction then the following proposition can be derived:

Proposition (Loury, 1978):
At each instant of time along an optimal program $C^*(t)$ for (46)''' discounted marginal utility must equal the expectation of discounted total utility at the end of the period under consideration.
The expectation is formed with respect to the distribution of T under the condition T>t; i.e.

$$e^{-rt}U'(C^*(t)) = E(e^{-rt}\frac{U(C^*(t))}{C^*(t)} | T>t),$$

where the conditional expectation is formed with using the distribution function $G_{C^*}(T)$.
Obviously an optimal policy depends on the discount factor, the utility function, and the distribution of Z.

II.2.4.2 Example with Exponentially Distributed Z

If Z is assumed to be exponentially distributed (see also II.1.2.2), i.e.

$$1 - F(x) = e^{-\lambda x} \quad , \quad \lambda > 0 \; ,$$

then the optimal extraction path is constant during the whole period under consideration, independent on the utility function and the discount factor. Obviously this example is of minor interest, too, and listed for completeness only.

II.2.5 Pure Competition and Optimal Extraction.

Subsequently a random resource stock size in pure competition will be discussed. The main issue is whether the market accomplishes optimal depletion, a fact, which was accomplished for the deterministic problem in chapter I.
Suppose, there is a great number of identical consumers and a great number of identical suppliers, competing with each others.
Initially each consumer has the same income at his disposal and can decide, how to purchase the natural resource or other commodities. Marginal utility of the other commodities is assumed to be constant. Each supplier has the same yet unknown initial amount of his own. Let us further assume that the resource cannot be stored so that the suppliers only have precise knowledge about the size of their part of the resource, when it is totally used up. Up to exhaustion only a probability distribution function of the resource, pertaining to exhaustion, is known.
Let $p(x;t)$ denote the price per unit of the resource, dependent on the quantity of the resource, used up until time t is reached.
Then each producer has the following optimization problem:
Maximize

$$J = \int_0^\infty p(x(t),t)C(t)dt$$

subject to

$$x(0) = 0 \; , \quad \dot{x}(t) = C(t) \; , \quad C(t) \geq 0.$$

Let $M := \sup\{x|F(x)<1\}$; if M is finite, then there can exist an equilibrium price only then, if $p(x;t) \equiv 0$ holds for $x > M$. Further an equilibrium price must fulfil $p(x,t) > 0$ for $x < M$, no matter, if M is finite or not. I.e. the suppliers can maximize their profits only if

$$M = \lim_{t\to\infty} x(t)$$

holds.

On consumer's side we have the optimization problem of maximizing

$$J = \int_0^\infty \lfloor e^{-rt}U(C(t))(1-F(x(t)))-p(x(t),t)C(t)\rfloor dt$$

with respect to x(t) and C(t).

The conditions for an equilibrium are

$$\frac{d}{dt}\lfloor e^{-rt}U'(C(t))(1-F(x(t)))\rfloor = -e^{-rt}U(C(t))f(x(t))$$

and

$$\lim_{t\to\infty} x(t) = M.$$

In summary we have the following

Proposition:

If there exists a solution of the optimization problem (46), then there also exists a market equilibrium, and this equilibrium coincides with the optimal allocation of the resource.

II.3 Optimal Extraction Rates and Unknown Costs of the Development of a Substitute

Until now we discussed two kinds of randomness with respect to the depletion of an exhaustible resource:

(1) The point of time, when a substitute of an exhaustible resource will be available, is unknown.
(2) The size of the total amount of the resource is unknown.

Subsequently we will discuss a third kind of randomness, which in a way is the reversal of (1):

(3) The point of time, when a substitute will be available, is known, yet the costs of developping this substitute are not known. This issue was examined more closely by Hoel (1978c, 1980).

II.3.1 One-period Analysis and Monopoly

Enlarging the notation, let y(t) denote the production rate of the substitute and c the (unknown) production costs of this commodity; extraction costs will not be taken into account. For the production costs c we initially only know the probability distribution function, and there will be no further information available until time T, when the substitute will have been developped.
Formally, we have the optimization problem of maximizing

$$E(W) := E(\int_0^\infty e^{-rt}[U(q(t)+y(t)-cy(t)]dt) ,$$

subject to

$$\dot{x}(t) = -q(t) , \quad x(0) = x^0$$
$$x(t) \geq 0,\ q(t) \geq 0,\ y(t) \geq 0, \text{and } y(t) = 0 \text{ for } t < T.$$

For the utility function U assume again the usual properties $U' > 0$ and $U'' < 0$.
If one fixes the reserves, which will be left at time T, then this optimization problem can be divided into two deterministic subproblems.

First the ante switch problem

$$F(S) := \max_{q} \int_{0}^{T} e^{-rt} U(q(t))dt$$

subject to

$$\dot{x}(t) = -q(t),\ x(0) = x^0,\ x(t) \geq 0,\ q(t) \geq 0$$

and secondly the post switch problem

$$G(S,c) := \max_{q,y} \int_{T}^{\infty} e^{-rt} \lfloor U(q(t)+y(t)) - cy(t) \rfloor dt$$

subject to

$$\dot{x}(t) = -q(t),\ x(0) = x^0,\ x(t) \geq 0,\ q(t) \geq 0, \text{and } x(T) = S.$$

Consequently S denotes the size of the remaining resource stock at time T.
For the optimal extraction path during period $\lfloor 0,T \rfloor$, denoted by $\tilde{q}(t,S)$, Hotelling's rule applies, i.e. $U(\tilde{q}(t,S))$ increases according to the discount rate r.
Let $\hat{q}(t,S,c)$ denote the optimal extraction path and $\hat{y}(t,S,c)$ the optimal production path after time T. Further let N(S,c) denote the point of time, when the resource will be totally depleted.
For the period (T,N(S,c)) one derives $\hat{y}(t,S,c) = 0$, and for $\hat{q}(t,S,c)$ once again Hotelling's rule holds. Further, N(S,c) can be obtained by the equation

$$U'(\hat{q}(t,S,c)) = c.$$

For t>N(S,c) evidently $q(\hat{t},S,c) = 0$ and $\hat{y}(t,S,c)$ satisfies the condition $\hat{y}(t,S,c) = k(c)$, where k(c) can be determined by the functional equation $U'(k(c)) = c$.
During the period $\lfloor 0,T \rfloor$ one obtains by Hotelling's rule

$$F'(S) = -e^{-rt} U'(\tilde{q}(t,S)) < 0$$

and during period $\lfloor T,N(S,c) \rfloor$

$$G_S'(S,c) = e^{-rt} U'(\hat{q}(t,S,c)) > 0 .$$

The problem of determining optimal reserves S^* leads to the following optimization problem:

Maximize

$$E(W) = F(S) + E(G(S,c))$$

subject to

$$S \geq 0 \quad \text{and} \quad S \leq x^0 .$$

For an optimal reserve $S = S^*$ this yields

$$F'(S^*) + E(G_S(S^*,c)) \leq 0,$$

where equality holds, if $S^* \neq 0$ holds.

Although the objective function of this optimization problem is concave with respect to q+y, it is linear with respect to the costs. But since uncertainty is only related to the costs, the expected value of the utility W, given q and y, only depends on the expected value of the costs c, which we denote by $\bar{c}$. In accordance to Hoel (1981) we call the economy risk neutral, if the objective function above is applied, and we call it risk averse, if the costs are assumed higher than $\bar{c}$ during the period after N(S,c). In this latter case one derives the following

<u>Proposition (Hoel, 1981):</u>

$S^* = 0$:

It is optimal to use up the whole resource stock during the period $\lfloor 0,T \rfloor$, if and only if it would be optimal, too, if costs would be known and are equal to $\bar{c}$.

If the whole resource stock will be exhausted at time T, the extraction path q(t) is independent on whether these costs are known or uncertain.

$S^* > 0$:

If it is optimal to leave reserves for time $t > T$, then the optimal extraction path will be at a lower level during period $\lfloor 0,T \rfloor$, if the economy behaves risk averse. If risk aversion is "high enough" then the optimal extraction path will be at a lower level for all $t \in \lfloor 0,T \rfloor$, if c is unknown, than it would be, if c would be known.

II.3.2 One-period Analysis and Pure Competition

In the subsequent section we will extend the preceding analysis to many identical decision makers, i.e. the market is assumed to be purely competitive.
Let the preferences of the consumers be given by the utility function $U(q(t))$, then for the price p in market equilibrium we must have

$$p(t) = U'(q(t)+y(t)) \ .$$

Moreover, according to Hotelling's rule, price p must rise proportional to the discount rate r, before time T is reached.
This yields

$$p(t) = U'(x(t,S)) \quad \text{for} \quad t < T \ .$$

Analogously one derives

$$p(t) = U'(\hat{q}(t,S,c)) \quad \text{for} \quad t \in (T,N(S,c)) \text{ and}$$
$$p(t) = c \quad \text{for} \quad t > N(S,c).$$

Obviously p(t) is not continuous at point T, unless there is a specific realization of the random variable c.
Related to the market equilibrium for optimal reserves S* the equation

$$F'(\bar{S}^*) + E(G_S(\bar{S}^*,c)) = 0$$

applies.
In summary we obtain the following

<u>Proposition (Hoel,1981):</u>

If all consumers and all suppliers of the resource behave risk neutral, then extraction of the resource as well as production of the substitute is optimal in market equilibrium.
If the consumers and/or suppliers of the resource behave risk averse in equilibrium, the extraction path during period $[0,T]$ is on a higher level than if c would be known, except of case $S^* = 0$. Hence there will be no extraction after time T.

II.3.3 Two-period Analysis

In generalization to sections 3.1 and 3.2 we will discuss now a model with linked consecutive periods. The end of the first period is assumed to be the point of breakthrough, when a new technology for production of a substitute of the exhaustible resource will be available.

The general results will be discussed for two subcases, for linear and log-linear demand functions.

The following assumptions are made:

Suppose, there is an economy, which produces one good, which can be produced by capital input $K(t)$ and input of the resource and/or the substitute, $q(t) + y(t)$, and primary factors, which are given exogenously. The aggregate commodity can be used for consumption, for the increase of the capital stock, for resource extraction, or for production of the substitute. Let further denote c_1 and c_2 the costs per unit of resource extraction and production of the substitute, respectively.

Let Φ denote the corresponding production function; hence

$$C(t) + K(t) + c_1 q(t) + c_2 y(t) = \Phi(K(t), q(t)+y(t), t) \qquad (55)$$

holds.

II.3.3.1 Optimal Extraction and one Decision Maker

II.3.3.1.1 Basic Model

Now the optimization problem is to determine a triple $(\hat{K}, \hat{q}, \hat{y})$ so that

$$W = \Psi(C(t))$$

will be maximal subject to (55) and some further constraints, specified below.

Ψ denotes an arbitrary strictly monotonically increasing function. Independent from the specification of the function Ψ, for an optimal solution $(\hat{K}, \hat{q}, \hat{y})$ we have the following inequality:

$$J(\hat{q}(t),\hat{y}(t)) \geq J(q(t),y(t))$$

for all admissible q(t) and y(t), where

$$J(q(t),y(t)) := \int_0^T e^{-\int_0^t r(\tau)d\tau} \left[\Phi(K(t),q(t)+y(t),t)-c_1 q(t)-c_2 y(t)\right]dt$$

and

$$r(\tau) := \frac{\partial\Phi(K(t),q(t)+y(t),t)}{\partial K}$$

hold.

Furthermore, it is assumed that market clearing will occur at each point of time, i.e. we have the demand function

$$h(p) = q(t)+y(t)$$

or by inversion

$$p(t) = h^{-1}(q(t)+y(t)).$$

We also have by maximizing the profit of the suppliers, taking price strategies

$$p(t) = \frac{\partial\Phi(K(t),q(t)+y(t),t)}{\partial(q(t)+y(t))} .$$

With z(t) := q(t)+y(t) both price functions coincide, if and only if

$$\Phi_{zK}\frac{dK(t)}{dt}\Big|_{K=\hat{K}} + \Phi_{zt} = 0 \qquad \text{for all z and t.}$$

For simplification assume further that the discount rate r(t) is independent of z; then, obviously, $\Phi_{zK} = 0$ and hence $\Phi_{zt} = 0$. Then the production function Φ must be separable:

$$\Phi(K,z,t) = \alpha(K,t)+\phi(z).$$

Hence

$$p(t) = h^{-1}(z) = \phi'(z)$$

and

$$r(t) = \frac{\partial \alpha(K(t),t)}{\partial K}\Big|_{K=\hat{K}} .$$

These simplifications lead to the objective function $J = Z + Z^0$ with

$$Z := \int_0^T e^{-rt}[\phi(q(t)+y(t))-c_1 q(t)-c_2 y(t)]dt$$

and

$$Z^0 := \int_0^T e^{-rt}\alpha(\hat{K}(t),t)dt.$$

Moreover, if K is given exogenously, the optimization problem reduces to the maximization of Z.

The amount of the exhaustible resource is assumed to be small enough so that it will be used up during the two periods under consideration. The subsequent inequality represents a sufficient condition for exhaustion:

$$\phi'(\frac{x^0}{2}) + \frac{x^0}{2}\phi''(\frac{x^0}{2}) > c_1 .$$

Once again, x^0 denotes the initial amount of the resource, and the inequality above only makes sense, if x^0 is known.

In order to obtain more specific results, let us now assume that x^0 is still known, yet initially for the production of the substitute it is only known that it will not be available during the first period and will be available during the second period with probability π.

At the beginning of the second period it is known, whether it will become available or not.

There is only a single decision maker, who controls the extraction of the resource. For simplicity $c_1 = 0$ (zero extraction costs) are assumed.

Then we have the objective function

$$Z = \phi(q(t)) + \frac{1}{1+r}[\phi(x^0-q(t)+y(t)-c_2 y(t)],$$

where $q(t)$ denotes resource extraction during the first period, $x_0-q(t)$ resource extraction during the second period, and $y(t)$ denotes the rate of production of the substitute.
Obviously we have the following implications:

$$y(t) \equiv 0 \quad \text{, if the new technology will not become available}$$

$$y(t) = \hat{y}(q(t)) \text{ , if the new technology will become available.}$$

By the objective function one derives

$$\phi'(x^0-q(t)+\hat{y}(q(t))) = c_2' \quad \text{for } \hat{y} \not\equiv 0. \tag{56}$$

Since the substitute availability is initially unknown, we have to maximize the following expectation:

$$(1+r)E(Z) = (1+r)\phi(q(t)) + \pi(\phi(x^0-q(t)+\hat{y}(q(t))-c_2\hat{y}(q(t))) +$$

$$+ (1-\pi)\phi(x^0-q(t)).$$

Since $(1+r)E(Z)$ is concave in q, one derives the following necessary and sufficient condition for an optimal extraction path q^*

$$(1+r)\phi'(q^*(t)) = f(q^*,\pi) \text{ or}$$

$$q^*(t) = \begin{cases} 0 & \text{and } (1+r)\phi'(0) < f(0,\pi) \\ & \text{or} \\ x^0 & \text{and } (1+r)\phi'(x^0) > f(x^0,\pi) \end{cases}$$

with

$$f(q,\pi) := \pi c_2 + (1-\pi)\phi'(x^0-q(t)). \tag{57}$$

II.3.3.1.2 Example with Linear Demand

For illustration assume a linear demand function

$$p = a - bq(t) \; ; \quad a,b>0. \tag{58}$$

This yields

$$\phi'(q(t)) = a - bq(t) \qquad (q < \frac{a}{b}) \tag{56'}$$

and hence

$$\phi(q(t)) = aq(t) - (1/2)bq^2(t).$$

The optimal extraction rate is now given by

$$\hat{q}(t) = \frac{ra+\pi(a-c_2)+(1-\pi)bx^0}{(2+r-\pi)b}. \tag{59}$$

II.3.3.2 Optimal Extraction and Pure Competition

The results of the preceding section will now be extended to identical suppliers of a competitive market.
Let $V^I(q)$ denote the discounted profit of a supplier in case that a new technology related to the production of a substitute will become available during the second period, and $V^{II}(q)$ the discounted profit in case that the technology will not become available.
Then the optimization problem of a typical supplier is to maximize the expected profits

$$E(U(V)) := \pi U(V^I(q)) + (1-\pi)U(V^{II}(q)).$$

The utility function U is assumed to be twice differentiable with $U' > 0$ and $U'' < 0$.
Necessary and sufficient conditions for $E(U(V))$ to be maximized by $\hat{q}(t)$ are

$$\pi U'(VI(q))\frac{dV^I(q)}{dq}+(1-\pi U'(V^{II}(q))\frac{dV^{II}(q)}{dq} = 0$$

or

$$\pi U'(V^I(0))\frac{dV^I(0)}{dq}+(1-\pi U'(V^{II}(0))\frac{dV^{II}(0)}{dq} < 0 \text{ and } q = 0$$

or

$$\pi U'(VI(S))\frac{dV^I(S)}{dq}+(1-\pi U'(V^{II}(S))\frac{dV^{II}(S)}{dq} > 0 \text{ and } q = S.$$

The discounted profit of a resource supplier is given by

$$V = p(1)q + (1/(1+r))p(2)(S-q), \tag{60}$$

where p(1), the price during the first period, as well as p(2), the price during the second period, are not influenced by the actions of the suppliers (assumption of pure competition). However, there is uncertainty about p(2), since it is not known whether the new technology will be available.
Now define a function $\pi^*(q)$ by

$$\frac{\pi^*(q)}{1-\pi^*(q)} = \frac{\pi U'(V^I(q))}{(1-\pi)U'(V^{II}(q))}.$$

Then the expected profits can be written

$$E(V^*) := p(1)q + \frac{1}{1+r}(S-q)(\pi^* p^I(2)+(1-\pi^*)p^{II}(2)). \tag{60$'$}$$

Here $p^I(2)$ denotes the price during the second period, if the substitute can be produced, and $p^{II}(2)$ the price during the second period, if the substitute cannot be produced.
Necessary and sufficient for this expected value to be maximal subject to a $q \in (0,S]$ is the following condition:

$$\pi^* p^I(2) + (1-\pi^*)p^{II}(2) = (1+r)p(1). \tag{61}$$

Assuming a linear demand function (i.e. (56)), the equilibrium price is determined by

$$p(1) = \phi'(q),$$

while the equilibrium price during the second period depends on whether the substitute can be produced or not, i.e. either

$$p^{II}(2) = \varphi'(S-q), \quad \text{(without production)}$$

or

$$p^{I}(2) = c \qquad \text{(with production)}.$$

Hence we have (see above (61))

$$\pi^*c + (1-\pi^*)\varphi'(S-q) = (1+r)\varphi'(q). \tag{61)'$$

If $\pi^* = \pi$, cases 3.3.1 and 3.3.2 agree, i.e. equation (61) coincides with the market equilibrium.

II. 3.3.3 Extraction of the Resource and Production of the Substitute by Exactly One Monopoly

Finally we will analyze optimal extraction, if a single decision maker controls the extraction of an exhaustible resource and the production of a substitute. Once again there is uncertainty, whether the substitute can be produced.

The decision maker's problem is as follows:

Maximize

$$E(V^*) = \pi^*V^{I}(q) + (1-\pi^*)V^{II}(q) \tag{60)"$$

with

$$V^{I}(q) = q\phi'(q) + \frac{1}{1+r}m(q),$$

where

$$m(q) := \max_{y>0} \left[(S-q+y)\phi'(S-q+y)-c_2y\right],$$

and

$$V^{II}(q) = q\phi'(q) + \frac{1}{1+r}\phi'(S-q). \tag{61)"$$

Since the monopolist tries to keep y = 0 - otherwise he would remain sitting on his reserves of the exhaustible resource - the inequality

$m(q) \geq \phi(S-q)$ must apply, and there is equality, if and only if marginal revenue at the beginning of the period, when the substitute will be produced, does not exceed the production costs, i.e.

$$m(q) = \phi'(S-q) \iff \phi'(S-q)+(S-q)\phi''(S-q) \leq c_2 .$$

<u>Case 1:</u> $m(q) = \phi'(S-q)$

For optimal extraction the following condition must apply:

$$(1+r)\lfloor \phi'(\hat{q})+\hat{q}\phi''(\hat{q}) \rfloor = \phi'(S-\hat{q})+(S-\hat{q})\phi''(S-\hat{q}).$$

Since $r \geq 0$ and $q\phi'(q)$ are strictly concave with respect to q, $\hat{q} \geq S/2$ must hold, and there is equality, if and only if $r = 0$.

<u>Case 2:</u> $m(q) > \phi'(S-q)$

For the monopolist it is profitable to use the new technology, and hence $m'(q) = -c_2$ holds.

Then we have the optimality condition

$$(1+r)\lfloor \phi'(\hat{q})+\hat{q}\phi''(\hat{q}) \rfloor = \tilde{f}(q,\pi^*), \tag{62}$$

where

$$\tilde{f}(q,\pi^*) := \pi^* c_2+(1-\pi^*)\lfloor \phi'(S-\hat{q})+(S-\hat{q})\phi''(S-\hat{q}) \rfloor .$$

Example (linear demand):

For illustration we once again assume a linear demand function (see (58)). Then condition (62) for optimal extraction yields

$$\hat{q} = \frac{ra+2bS}{(2+r)2b}, \qquad (\hat{q} \leq S), \quad a-2b(S-\hat{q}) \leq c_2 . \tag{59$'$}$$

Inserting q into the latter inequality one obtains a necessary and sufficient optimality condition for $\hat{q}$:

$$a - \frac{2+r}{2+2r} c_2 \leq bS.$$

If this inequality is violated, a solution is given by

$$\hat{q} = \frac{ra+\pi^*(a-c_2)+(1-\pi^*)2bS}{(2+r-\pi^*)2b} \qquad (\hat{q} < S). \qquad (59)''$$

I.e. the optimal extraction path in case of pure competition coincides with monopolistic extraction, if $r = \pi^* = 0$ and consequently $\hat{q} = S$. Otherwise monopolistic extraction will be lower than competitive extraction during the whole first period.

If only the extraction of the resource is controlled by a monopolist and the production of the substitute is left to many (identical) decision makers, competing with each others, one obtains the same result, except $\hat{q} < \tilde{q}$ holds, where $\tilde{q}$ is given by

$$\bar{q} = 0 \qquad , \text{ if } \phi'(S) > c_2 \text{ or}$$

$$\phi'(S-\bar{q}) = c_2 \quad , \text{ if } \phi'(S) < c_2 .$$

In this case the optimal extraction path is given by $\bar{q}$.

If the size of the resource stock is unknown, similar results can be derived analogously.

II.4 Conclusions

In this chapter three kinds of uncertainty, related to the depletion of an exhaustible resource are discussed.
First it is assumed that research and development of a future technology is done in order to replace the exhaustible resource, which is essential for a certain production process.
In the model of Dasgupta and Heal (1974), discussed first, technical progress, i.e. research and development of a new production technology for a substitute of the exhaustible resource, was assumed to be exogenously given.
Uncertainty was related to the point of time, when a new production technology or a substitute of the resource is found, and consequently the resource becomes inessential.
The next model, an extension of Dasgupta's and Heals's, was to model

technical progress to be endogenous, as worked out by Kamien and Schwartz (1978). The intensity of research and development of a new technology can be controlled and consequently the point of time, when the new technology breakthrough occurs, is still random, yet influenced by the policies of the decision makers.
The second kind of uncertainty discussed, was given by unknown size of the resource.
A model of Pan-Tai Liu (1980) was analyzed with respect to monopolistic and pure competitive market structure, related to consumer's view and to the issue, whether the market will enforce optimal depletion. In case of the existence of an optimal policy, this policy coincides with market equilibrium.
The third kind of uncertainty is related to the first one, i.e. the point of time of technical breakthrough is known, yet the costs, which have to be spent to research and development of the new technology or a substitute of the exhaustible resource, are unknown.
Finally some models of different market structures of M. Hoel (1978c, 1980) are discussed.

III. SHORT INTRODUCTION TO THE THEORY OF DIFFERENTIAL GAMES

In order to prepare for the results of the two subsequent chapters, some definitions and important theorems of game theory are brought together (see e.g. A. Friedman, 1971).
Suppose, there is a system of differential equations

$$\dot{x} = f(t,x,u_1(t),u_2(t),\dots,u_N(t)) \quad , \quad t \in [0,T] \tag{1}$$
$$x(0) = x^0.$$

and let U_i $(i=1,2,\dots,N)$ denote compact subsets of the m_i-dimensional Euclidean spaces R^{m_i}. Then a measurable function $u_i(t)$, the values of which lie in U_i almost everywhere on $[0,T]$, is called a control function. A solution $x(t)$ of the system (1) is called a trajectory or a path, corresponding to the controls $u_1,u_2,\dots,u_N$. Further let the following payoff or cost functionals, respectively, of the players P_i $(i = 1,2,\dots,N)$ be given by:

$$J_i(u_1,\dots,u_N) = g_i(T,x(T)) + \int_0^T L_i(t,x,u_1,\dots,u_N)dt \qquad (i = 1,2,\dots,N) \tag{2}$$

$T = T(x)$ denotes the duration of the path $x(t)$, i.e. each player is to maximize (minimize) his objective functional.

Let $n \in \mathbb{N}$ be arbitrarily given and $\delta := \frac{T}{n}$, and let

$$I_j = (t_{j-1},t_j] \quad , \quad t_j = j\delta \tag{3}$$

be a partition of the interval $[0,T]$.
Let further $Z_j^{(k)}$ denote the control space on I_j.
Then we define the maps

$$\Gamma_{\delta,j}^{(k)}: Z_1^{(1)} \times Z_1^{(2)} \times\dots\times Z_1^{(N)} \times Z_2^{(1)} \times Z_2^{(2)} \times\dots\times Z_2^{(N)} \times\dots$$
$$\dots\times Z_{j-1}^{(1)}\times Z_{j-1}^{(2)}\times\dots\times Z_{j-1}^{(N)} \to Z_j^{(k)} , \quad 2\le j\le n. \tag{4}$$

Each element contained in $Z_1^{(k)}$ let be denoted by $\Gamma_{\delta,1}^{(k)}$, since there exists no map into $Z_1^{(k)}$.

Then the vector

$$\Gamma_\delta^{(k)} = (\Gamma_{\delta,1}^{(k)},\dots,\Gamma_{\delta,n}^{(k)}) \tag{5}$$

is called a lower δ-strategy of player P_k, and the vector

$$\Gamma_\delta = (\Gamma_\delta^{(1)},\dots,\Gamma_\delta^{(N)}) \tag{6}$$

is called a lower δ-strategy for $P = (P_1,P_2,\dots,P_N)$.
For each lower δ-strategy there exist uniquely determined controls u_k $(k=1,2,\dots,N)$ with components $u_{k,j}$ on I_j:

$$\begin{aligned} u_{k,1} &= \Gamma_{\delta,1}^{(k)} \\ u_{k,j} &= \Gamma_{\delta,j}^{(k)}(u_{1,1},\dots,u_{N,1},\dots,u_{1,j-1},\dots,u_{N,j-1}). \end{aligned} \tag{7}$$

By the vector $u = (u_1,\dots,u_N)$ a trajectory $x(t)$ is determined according to the state equation (1).
Controls u jointly with the corresponding trajectory x determine the outcomes $J_i(u_1,\dots,u_N)$.

Definition (Differential Game):
Let $G(\delta)$ denote the scheme (3) - (6) of lower δ-strategies Γ_δ of P and let $J(u)$ be the corresponding payoffs, then the sequence

$$G = \{G(\delta)\} \quad (\delta = \frac{T}{n}\,; \quad n = 1,2,\dots)$$

is called a differential game with respect to system (1) and outcome (2).
A sequence $\Gamma^{(k)} = \{\Gamma_\delta{}^{(k)}\}$ is called a strategy of player P_k.
A vector $\Gamma = (\Gamma(1),\dots,\Gamma(N))$, the components $\Gamma^{(k)}$ of which are strategies of P_k, is called a strategy of P $(k = 1,2,\dots,N)$.

Definition (Nash-equilibrium):
A strategy $\Gamma^* = (\Gamma^{*(1)},\dots,\Gamma^{*(N)})$ is called an equilibrium point or an equilibrium strategy of the differential game G, if

$$J_k(\Gamma^{*(1)},\dots,\Gamma^{*(k-1)},\Gamma^{(k)},\Gamma^{*(k+1)},\dots,\Gamma^{*(N)}) \leq J(\Gamma^*)$$

holds for all strategies $\Gamma^{(1)},\dots,\Gamma^{(N)}$ and $k = 1,2,\dots,N$.

According to relation (7) between strategies and controls, the definition of an equilibrium can be formulated equivalently in terms of the control functions $u_1,\ldots,u_N$.
An equilibrium does not necessarily need to be optimal for all players as well. It is possible that each player could receive a better result, if one or more of them would move away from this equilibrium e.g. by cooperation, i.e. there can exist points, which dominate a Nash equilibrium point (see e.g. the so-called "prisoner's dilemma").

There are two kinds of control functions:

1. Open-loop controls:

The control functions u_i only depend on time:

$$u_i = u_i(t) \quad (i=1,2,\ldots N). \tag{8}$$

Analogously to Optimal Control Theory one can derive necessary conditions for $(u_1{}^*,u_2{}^*,\ldots,u_N{}^*)$ to be an open-loop Nash equilibrium. For that purpose one uses the N Hamiltonian functions

$$H_i = L_i + (\lambda_i, f) - (\mu_i, \Phi_i), \quad (i=1,2,\ldots,N),$$

where $(\cdot,\cdot)$ denotes the inner product, and Φ_i represents the constraints due to the control and/or state variables.

Theorem (Case, 1969):
The following conditions are necessary for $(u_1{}^*,u_2{}^*,\ldots,u_N{}^*)$ to be an open-loop Nash equilibrium point:

1. There exist non-trivial solutions of the differential equations

$$\dot{\lambda}_i = -\frac{\partial H_i{}^*}{\partial x} + \lambda_i \quad , \quad (t \in [0,\infty),\ i=1,2,\ldots,N), \tag{9}$$

where $H_i{}^*$ denotes the Hamiltonian at the point $(u_1{}^*,\ldots,u_N{}^*)$;

2. $(\mu_i,\Phi_i) = 0$ if $\mu_i(t) > 0$, $(i=1,2,\ldots,N)$; (10)
3. $u_i{}^*$ maximizes $H_i(t,x(t),u_1{}^*,\ldots,u_{i-1}{}^*,u_i,u_{i+1}{}^*,\ldots,u_N{}^*)$ with respect to u_i for all $i = 1,2,\ldots,N$; (11)
4. $\lim\limits_{t\to\infty} \lambda_i(t) = 0$, $(i=1,2,\ldots,N)$. (12)

2. Closed-loop controls:

The control functions u_i do depend on time and the trajectory $x(s)$, $s \leq t$:

$$u_i = u_i(t,(x(s),\ 0 \leq s \leq t)). \qquad (8)'$$

Since in deterministic games past states can be subsumed into the present state, (8)′ can be rewritten shorter

$$u_i = u_i(t,x(t)). \qquad (8)''$$

In order not to exclude bang-bang controls, the values of which lie on the boundary of the control region, discontinuous control functions must be admitted. This, however, means that the partial differential equation

$$\dot{x}(t) = f(t,x(t),u_1(t,x(t)),\ldots,u_N(t,x(t))) \qquad (1)'$$

can have a discontinuous right-hand side.

Disregarding the problem of the existence of a closed-loop equilibrium we have the following

Theorem (Case, 1969):

The following conditions are sufficient for $(u_1^*(t,x),\ldots u_N^*(t,x))$ to be a closed-loop Nash equilibrium:

1. u_i^* are piecewise regular with respect to (t,x), $(i=1,2,\ldots,N)$;
2. In each region D, where u_i^* $(i=1,2,\ldots,N)$ are regular, there exists a non-trivial solution of the differential equation

$$\dot{\lambda}_i = -\frac{\partial H_i^*}{\partial x} + \lambda_i \qquad (i=1,2,\ldots,N) \qquad (9)'$$

3. $(\mu_i,\Phi_i) = 0$ for all $(t,x) \in D$, $\mu_i \geq 0$; $(i=1,2,\ldots,N)$ (10)′

4. u_i^* maximizes $H_i(t,x,u_1^*,\ldots,u_{i-1}^*,u_i,u_{i+1}^*,\ldots,u_N^*)$ for all $(t,x) \in D$; (11)′

5. $\lim_{t\to\infty} \lambda_i(t) = 0$ $(i=1,2,\ldots,N)$ and $\lim_{t\to\infty} x(t) = 0$ (12)′

Note that the equations (9)′ and the state equation (1)′ are partial differential equations.
In both cases, open-loop and closed-loop controls, the equations (1), (9), and (10), or (1)′, (9)′, and (10)′, respectively, form a system of N+1 non-linear differential equations with two boundary conditions, i.e. we have a two point boundary value problem. Generally there exist no analytic solution of such problems.

IV. DYNAMIC MODELS OF RESOURCE EXTRACTION AND DUOPOLISTIC MARKETS

This chapter introduces some models of oligopolistic markets for finite, nonrenewable depletable natural resources. Only oligopolistic models with a game theoretical approach are analyzed. A distinction is made between models with discrete time parameter and with continuous time parameter on the one hand, and between closed-loop controls and open-loop controls on the other hand. In case of closed-loop controls each oligopolist or player can redecide on his future strategy in considering the state of the game at each instant of time. In case of open-loop control the players can "only have a look at the watch", i.e. they cannot reconsider the state of the game and consequently they have to fix their strategies at initial time for the whole period under consideration.

In case of quantity strategies the amount $x(t)$ of the resource, still available at time t, is the state variable and the extraction rate $q(t)$ the control variable. In case of price strategies the prices, fixed by the oligopolists, are the control variables, and the state $x(t)$ is determined by the extraction rates $q_i(t)$ corresponding to the prices $p_i(t)$ as given by the demand function.

Assuming the extractable resource to be a homogeneous good, in case of price strategies the initial endowments of the resource play an important role, hence the discussion of asymmetric oligopolies, i.e. nonsymmetrically endowed oligopolies, is of interest.

The solution concept chosen is the non-cooperative Nash equilibrium. Although this concept implies some shortcomings (changes of the strategy of one player are compared to each others isolated from joint changes of the strategies of all other players) it makes economically sense. Once reached, a Nash point is stable, since sliding away from it, a player has to expect a worse result. Therefore it is a sensible setup in our context, since we assume that all suppliers compete with one another, or, if they form a cartel, this cartel competes with those suppliers, who do not participate at the cartel.

Although Stackelberg solutions in particular for asymmetric oligopolies could be of interest, they are not analyzed. Stackelberg equilibria are dynamically inconsistent in the sense that they depend on the initial point of time: Suppose, a Stackelberg model is treated with initial time 0 and thereafter once again with initial time $t_0 > 0$ with values, given by the first solution at time t_0, then both solutions can differ from one another after time t_0 (see e.g. Simaan and Cruz, 1973b).

IV.1. An Introductory Duopoly Model with Production Strategies

For illustration we analyze a special case of a duopoly model of Burgermeister (see Krelle, 1976, pp.457). In accordance with our assumptions the commodity supplied, cannot be steadily produced, yet is available at a finite amount.
Each duopolist i (i=1,2) can control his extraction rates $q_i(t)$, which he supplies. His initial endowments x_i^0 with the resource are given. Further there are restrictions related to the change of the control variables:

$$\sigma_i^- \leq \frac{dx_i(t)}{dt} \leq \sigma_i^+, \quad t \in \lfloor 0,T \rfloor .$$

The costs for the duopolists are given by

$$c_i(t) = c_i(\dot{x}_i(t)) = c_i(q_i(t));$$

i.e. each duopolist owns an initial endowment x_i^0 of the resource, which can be changed by extraction; in this case it can only be diminished. The smallest and greatest change are given by the resource restriction:

$$\sigma_i^- = 0 \text{ and } \sigma_i^+ = x_i(t), \quad (t \in \lfloor 0,T \rfloor ; \; i=1,2).$$

The costs are assumed to be independent on the remaining amount of the resource stock and are related to the extraction rate $q_i(t)$.

Example 1 (linear demand, linear costs):

For a special case of duopoly the model can be treated analytically as follows:

The common price p(t) is assumed to be linear in both extraction rates

$$p(t) = A-a(q_1(t)+q_2(t)) , \qquad A,a > 0 , \tag{1}$$

and the costs are likelwise assumed to be linear:

$$c_i(t) = bq_i(t) , \quad b > 0. \tag{2}$$

Each duopolist's objective is to maximize his discounted profit over period $\lfloor 0,T \rfloor$:

$$\int_0^T \lfloor q_i(t)(A-a(q_1(t)+q_2(t))) - bq_i(t) \rfloor e^{rt}dt \to \max \; (i=1,2).$$

By Pontrjagin's maximum principle one derives the necessary conditions

$$\ell_i(q_1,q_2,t) := \int_{t'}^T \lfloor -2aq_i(t)-aq_j(t)+A \rfloor e^{-rt}dt$$

and hence the equilibrium strategies are

$$q_i(t') = \begin{cases} 0, & \text{if } \ell_i < b\, e^{-rt} \\ \sigma_i^+ = x_i(t), & \text{if } \ell_i > b\, e^{-rt} \end{cases} \qquad (i=1,2) \tag{3}$$

for all $t' \in \lfloor 0,T \rfloor$, for which $q_i(t') = \dot{x}_i(t')$.
This result of Burgermeister can be obtained by differential game theory as follows:

Example 2 (Differential game theory analysis of example 1):

Let the market of an exhaustible resource be described by the following differential game: Each duopolist owns an initial amount x_i^0 of the resource, which cannot be enlarged during the interval under consideration$\lfloor 0,T \rfloor$, it only can be reduced by extraction. The extraction rate is assumed to be the only control variable of each duopolist.

I.e the differential game is governed by the state equations

$$\dot{x}_i = -q_i(t)\ , \quad x_i(0) = x_i^0\ ; \quad i = 1,2\ ; \quad t \in [0,T].$$

Once again let the demand function be given by equation (1), but the extraction costs are assumed to depend on the remaining reserves of the duopolists:

$$c_i = B - bx(t)\ ; \quad B,b > 0\ ; \quad x(t) := x_1(t) + x_2(t). \qquad (2)'$$

This can be interpreted as follows: There is a common pool of the resource and both duopolists can extract the joint reserve; further it is assumed that those deposits of the common reserves, which can be exploited with low technical effort, are extracted first.
The duopolist's profit is given by

$$J_i(q_1,q_2) = \int_0^T q_i(t)[A-a(q_1(t)+q_2(t))-B+bx(t)]e^{-rt}dt \qquad (i=1,2)$$

$$=: \int_0^T L_i(q_1,q_2,x)dt.$$

Moreover, the following constraints on the control variables are given:

$$q_i(t) \leq x_i(t) \iff q_i(t)-x_i(t) \leq 0 \iff: D(x_i,q_i,t) \leq 0 \qquad (4)$$

Then we have the Hamiltonians

$$H_i = L_i-\lambda_i q_i+\mu_i(q_i-x_i)$$

$$=Aq_ie^{-rt}-Bq_ie^{-rt}+bq_ixe^{-rt}-aq_i^2e^{-rt}-aq_iq_je^{-rt}-$$

$$-\lambda_iq_i+\mu_iq_i-\mu_ix_i\ ; \quad i \neq j.$$

Hence one derives the following necessary conditions for the maximization of the duopolist's profits:

$$H_{q_i} = e^{-rt}(A-B+bx-2aq_i-aq_j) - \lambda_i + \mu_i; \quad i \neq j.$$

This yields

$$q_i(t) = \frac{A}{2a} - \frac{B}{2a} + \frac{b}{2a}x(t) - \frac{1}{2}q_j(t) - \frac{\lambda_i}{2a}e^{rt} + \frac{\mu_i}{2a}e^{rt} = 0. \qquad (5)$$

For the case D = 0 we also have the necessary condition

$$\frac{A}{2a} - \frac{B}{2a} + \frac{b}{2a}x(t) - x_i(t) - \frac{1}{2}q_i(t) - \frac{\lambda_i}{2a}e^{rt} + \frac{\mu_i}{2a}e^{rt} = 0; \quad i \neq j$$

and this yields

$$\mu_i = -Ae^{-rt}+Be^{-rt}-bx(t)e^{-rt}+2ax_i(t)e^{-rt}+aq_j(t)e^{-rt}+\lambda_i \qquad (6)$$

Inserting (6) into equation (5) one obtains

$$q_i(t) = x_i(t); \quad i \in \{1,2\} \qquad (3)'$$

and consequently by the state equation

$$q_i(t) = x_i^0 e^{-t} \; ; \quad i \in \{1,2\}.$$

1. This solution is obviously a bang-bang control, since it runs along the boundary of the feasible control region (4).
2. Although this example cannot give any empirical convincing answer, it shows that the differential game approach can be a powerful method to derive useful results with other assumptions, which are closer to reality.
3. The open-loop Nash equilibrium point can be interpreted as follows:

   By the choice of the linear demand and cost functions the profit of each supplier changes at each instant of time at the same proportion. Following the declining remaining amount of the resource the extraction costs rise for both suppliers. On the other hand the price rises proportionally (see (3)') according to the smaller extraction rates. Consequently one duopolist does not care about the other's activities. In each case it is best for the duopolists to supply as much as possible, i.e. as much as the resource restriction admits.

IV.2 Duopoly with Price Strategies and Exploration

Two suppliers of an exhaustible resource set the price of the resource, and demand is given by the equation

$$q_i = q_i(p_i(t), p_j(t), t) \; ; \qquad i \in \{1,2\} \; , \quad i \neq j \tag{7}$$

where

$$q_i = a_i p_i^{-\varepsilon_i} p_j^{\eta_i} \; ; \qquad a_i \in R \tag{7)'$$

or inverting the demand

$$p_i = q_i^{-(\varepsilon_j/D)} q_j^{-(\eta_i/D)} \; ; \qquad i \neq j \tag{7)"$$

with

$$\varepsilon_i > 0 \; , \quad \eta_i > 0 \text{, and} \quad D = \varepsilon_1 \varepsilon_2 - \eta_1 \eta_2 > 0.$$

Here ε_i denotes the elasticity of demand with respect to the price of duopolist i ($i \in \{1,2\}$), and η_j denotes the elasticity of demand with respect to the price of the other duopolist j ($j \neq i$). The parameter constraints are that the direct impact of changing the price of duopolist i is greater than the one of his competitor. Now, both duopolists are interested in maximizing their discounted profits

$$J_i = \int_0^\infty [(p_i - c_i) q_i(p_i, p_j) - v_i \ell_i] e^{-rt} dt \tag{8}$$

subject to the constraints

$$\begin{aligned} \dot{x}_i &= \ell_i - q_i \qquad \text{(state equations)} \\ x_i(0) &= x_i^0 \end{aligned} \tag{9}$$

$$\ell_i \geq 0 \text{ and } p_i \geq 0 \tag{10}$$

$$\ell_i \leq \frac{1}{v_i}(p_i - c_i) q_i(p_i, p_j) \; ; \quad \ell_i(t) = 0 \text{ for } t > T \tag{11}$$

$$q_i(p_i, p_j) \leq x_i, \tag{12}$$

where $\ell_i(t)$ denotes the exploration rate of duopolist i and $v_i(t)$ denotes the corresponding exploration costs per unit of the resource, found by exploration.
The state of this differential game is once again given by the remaining amounts of the resource or, in other words, the extraction capacities of the two players.
The control variables are the prices p_i and the exploration rates ℓ_i.

IV.2.1 Open-loop Controls

The Hamiltonians according to the differential game (8) - (12) are given by

$$H_i = (p_i-c_i)q_i-v_i\ell_i+\lambda_i(\ell_i-q_i)+\mu_i(\ell_j-q_j)+\nu_i(x_i-q_i). \tag{13}$$

From these Hamiltonians one derives the necessary conditions for optimality of p_i and ℓ_i:

$$\dot{\lambda}_i = r\lambda_i-\nu_i \tag{14}$$

$$\dot{\mu}_i = r\mu_i \tag{15}$$

$$(q_i+(p_i-c_i)\frac{\partial q_i}{\partial p_i})(1+\frac{1}{v_i}(p_i-v_i))-\nu_i\frac{\partial q_i}{\partial p_i} = 0 \tag{16}$$

$$\begin{aligned} \lambda_i-v_i > 0 &\iff \ell_i = \frac{1}{v_i}(p_i-c_i)q_i \\ \lambda_i = v_i \quad &\iff \ell_i > 0 \\ \lambda_i-v_i < 0 &\iff \ell_i = 0 \end{aligned} \tag{17}$$

$$\nu_i \geq 0,\ x_i-q_i \geq 0,\ \nu_i(x_i-q_i) = 0. \tag{18}$$

Obviously by assumption capacity constraints (12) as well as the financial constraints (11) (due to the exploratory effort), are only influenced by the duopolist's own actions.
The policies of the two players are ruled by equations (17) and (18).

Hence six cases are to be distinguished

1. $\nu_i = 0$ and $\lambda_i - v_i = 0$;
2. $\nu_i = 0$ and $\lambda_i - v_i > 0$;
3. $\nu_i = 0$ and $\lambda_i - v_i < 0$;
4. $\nu_i > 0$ and $\lambda_i - v_i < 0$ (policy 1);
5. $\nu_i > 0$ and $\lambda_i - v_i = 0$ (policy 2);
6. $\nu_i > 0$ and $\lambda_i - v_i > 0$ (policy 3).

Table 1 (Possible Nash Configurations)

The first and the second case can be excluded, since none of the duopolists will invest into exploration of new reserves as long as the capacity constraints are not binding.
Calculating optimal investment rates ℓ_i and optimal rates of the change of the prices $\pi_i = (\dot{p}_i/p_i)$, we will distinguish the four price levels:

$$p_i^* := \frac{\varepsilon_i}{\varepsilon_i - 1}((1+r)v_i + c_i) \tag{19}$$

$$\tilde{p}_i := v_i + c_i \qquad \text{(lowest price)} \tag{20}$$

$$\bar{p}_i := (1 + \frac{x_i}{\varepsilon_j})v_i + c_i \qquad \text{(mean price)} \tag{21}$$

$$\hat{p}_i := (1 + \frac{\varepsilon_i}{x_j})v_i + c_i \qquad \text{(highest price)} \tag{22}$$

For each price level the following inequalities hold:

$$\tilde{p}_i < p_i^* \quad \text{and} \quad \tilde{p}_i < \bar{p}_i < \hat{p}_i .$$

Using these notations we can describe all possible open-loop Nash equilibrium points: (The righthand side bracketts denote the respective policies of the duopolists (see Table 1 above).

$$(1\text{-}1) \qquad \begin{cases} \ell_i = 0 \ , & \pi_i = \dfrac{\varepsilon_j}{v_i D}\bar{p}_i \\ \ell_i = 0 \ , & \ell_i = (1/v_j)p_j x_j \end{cases}$$

$$(1\text{-}2) \qquad \pi_i = \frac{\varepsilon_j}{v_i D}\tilde{p}_i \ , \quad \pi_j = 0 \ , \quad p_j = p_j^*$$

$$(2\text{-}1) \qquad p_j^* > p_j > 0$$

$$(2\text{-}2) \qquad \begin{cases} \ell_i = (1/v_i)\tilde{p}_i x_j \\ \pi_i = 0 , \quad p_i = p_i^* \\ p_i > 0 \end{cases}$$

$$\begin{matrix}(3\text{-}1)\\(1\text{-}3)\end{matrix} \qquad \begin{cases} \ell_i = (1/v_i)p_i x_i , \quad \ell_j = 0 \\ \pi_i = \frac{\varepsilon_j}{v_i D}(\bar{p}_i - p_i) , \quad \pi_j = \frac{\eta_j}{v_i D}(\hat{p}_i - p_i) \end{cases}$$

$$\begin{matrix}(3\text{-}2)\\ \\(2\text{-}3)\end{matrix} \qquad \begin{cases} \ell_i = (1/v_i)p_i x_i , \quad \ell_j = \frac{\eta_j}{v_i \varepsilon_i}(\hat{p}_i - p_i)x_i \\ \pi_i = \frac{1}{v_i \varepsilon_i}(\tilde{p}_i - p_i) , \quad \pi_j = 0 , \quad p_j = p_j^* \\ p_i > \tilde{p}_i , \quad p_j^* > p_j , \quad p_i < \hat{p}_i \end{cases}$$

$$(3\text{-}3) \qquad \begin{cases} \ell_i = (1/v_i)p_i x_i \\ \pi_i = \frac{\varepsilon_j}{v_i D}(\tilde{p}_i - p_i) + \frac{\eta_i}{v_j D}(\tilde{p}_j - p_j) \end{cases}$$

For the construction of a Nash equilibrium we make the further assumptions:

(A1) At initial time the prices are set to a level that the extraction rate is given by $q_i(p_1{}^0, p_2{}^0) = x_i{}^0$ $(i=1,2)$.

(A2) For the initial prices $p_i{}^0 < p_i^*$ holds for all $i = 1,2$.

(A3) The multipliers of the Hamiltonians are continuous along an equilibrium path.

With these assumptions open-loop equilibrium paths are composed of the following types of trajectories (sequences of policy regimes):

s_1: (3-3) → (2-3) → (2-2)
s_2: (3-3) → (1-3) → (2-3) → (2-2)
s_3: (3-3) → (1-3) → (1-2) → (2-2)

No matter which path will be chosen, in each case it ends at the point (p_1^*, p_2^*) and with policy 2 for both duopolists.
However, this policy only holds until time T, when

$$\ell_i(t) = 0 \qquad \text{for all } t > T$$

(see (11)), since there are no more reserves to explore.
During the period $\lfloor 0,T \rfloor$ both duopolists' exploratory effort is as high as possible so that prices decline until time t*, when $p_i(t^*) = p_i^*(t^*)$ holds for each i = 1,2.
The curve in phase space, which represents this path, can be determined by the differential equation

$$\frac{dp_2}{dp_1} = \frac{p_2}{p_1} \cdot \frac{\frac{\varepsilon_1}{v_2}(\tilde{p}_2 - p_2) + \frac{\eta_2}{v_1}(\tilde{p}_1 - p_1)}{\frac{\varepsilon_2}{v_1}(\tilde{p}_1 - p_1) + \frac{\eta_1}{v_2}(\tilde{p}_2 - p_2)} \tag{23}$$

$$p_2(p_1^*) = p_2^*$$

This curve divides the phase space into two parts:

1. The region, where duopolist 1, applying policy 3, is able to reach price p_1^* before duopolist 2 can reach price p_2^*.
2. The mirror policy regime region, where duopolist 2 plays the role of 1 and 1 the role of 2.

Obviously it suffices to discuss one of these two symmetric cases. Let us analyze the first one.
We have to distinguish between two cases:

a) $\hat{p}_2 > p_2^0$: If price p_2 is higher than initial price p_2^0, then (2-3) is an admissible regime. Player 1 can pursue exploration, although his extraction rate decreases. The price, set by player 2, decreases. Hence the equilibrium is given by s_1. That means that both players initially adopt policy 3 (by assumption), where they pursue exploratory effort as high as possible. Hence the prices decrease, and the extraction rates increase until time t_1^* is reached, when p_1 will have reached price p_1^*. From then on player 1 applies policy 2; i.e. the price p_1^* is held constantly, and the extraction rate decreases, since further exploration takes place. The second player, however, further decreases the price and consequently increases his extraction rate until time t* is reached, when $p2 = p2^*$ holds, too. From then on both players apply their policy 2.

b) $\hat{p}_2 < p_2^0$: If $\hat{p}_2 < p_2^0$ holds, there are two possibilities:
Either we have the same equilibrium as in case a), or the following situation occurs:
Initially both players apply their policy 3. From a certain point of time on, say τ_1, player 1 stops his exploratory effort, though the price level p_1^* does not yet be reached. From then on p_2 declines. Parallel p_1 becomes lower than p_1^*. When price p_2 will have reached p_2^*, price p_1 begins to increase until it will reach p_1^* from below.
From then on two constellations can occur, depending on whether player 1 is able to hold price p_1 at the level p_1^*.
Consequently we have either paths s_2 or s_3.
Moreover, note that s_3 can never be an equilibrium, if $p_2^* < \bar{p}_2$, and s_2 can never be an equilibrium, if $p2^* > p2$ holds.

Obviously, in case of open-loop control the prices are the main control variables. The exploration rates are of minor importance.
Hence the extraction rates depend directly on the prices.
From time T on, when no longer exploration can take place, we have the situation of example 2 of IV.1 with exponentially decreasing extraction rates. The initial values x_i^T of the remaining resource stocks at time T can be determined by the state equation (9).

IV.2.2 Closed-loop Controls

The control variables are dependent on time and on the remaining reserves of the resource available to each player. Consequently prices and exploration rates, set by each duopolist, are functions of both, time and remaining resource amounts:

$$p_i = p_i(t,x_i,x_j) \qquad (i\varepsilon\{1,2\},\ i\neq j)$$
$$\ell_i = \ell_i(t,x_i,x_j).$$

The Hamiltonians of the corresponding optimization problem are given by

$$H_i = (p_i-c_i)q_i - v_i\ell_i - \lambda_i(\ell_i-q_i) + \mu_i(\ell_j-q_j)$$

and have to be maximized with respect to p_i and ℓ_i subject to constraint (11) and (12).
Since H_i is linear with respect to ℓ_i, we derive

$$\ell_i = \begin{cases} 0, & \text{if } \lambda_i < v_i \\ \text{undetermined}, & \text{if } \lambda_i = v_i \\ (1/v_i)(p_i-c_i)q_i, & \text{if } \lambda_i > v_i. \end{cases} \tag{24}$$

Maximizing H_i with respect to p_i we have to consider that constraint (12) is violated, if

$$q_i + (p_i-c_i)\frac{\partial q_i}{\partial p_i} < 0$$

holds.
This infeasibility can be avoided in assuming that the extraction rates are sufficiently small.
If extraction capacities are used up completely, one derives the following equilibrium prices, using the demand function (7)′:

$$p_i = x_i^{-(\varepsilon_j/D)} x_j^{-(\eta_i/D)}; \quad (i \neq j;\ i,j=1,2). \tag{7)'''$$

The corresponding exploration rates can be determined by inserting these prices into equation (24).
By Theorem 2 of chapter III we derive the subsequent sufficient conditions for a Nash equilibrium:

$$\dot{\lambda}_i = -(p_i-c_i) - \frac{\partial p_i}{\partial x_i}x_i - (\lambda_i-v_i)\frac{\partial \ell_i}{\partial x_i} + (1+r)\lambda_i - \mu_i\frac{\partial \ell_i}{\partial x_i}, \tag{25}$$

$$\dot{\mu}_i = - \frac{\partial p_i}{\partial x_j}x_i - (\lambda_i-v_i)\frac{\partial \ell_i}{\partial x_j} + ((1+r) - \frac{\partial \ell_j}{\partial x_j})\mu_i \tag{26}$$

where

$$\lim_{t\to\infty} \dot{\lambda}_i = \lim_{t\to\infty} \dot{\mu}_i = \lim_{t\to\infty} \dot{q}_i = 0. \tag{27}$$

Due to condition (27) the equilibrium strategy corresponds to policy (2-2), where $\lambda_i = v_i$ and $\ell_i = 0$ hold.
Consequently we can rewrite (27) as follows:

$$(1+r)v_i = (p_i-c_i) + \frac{\partial p_i}{\partial x_i}x_i; \qquad (i \in \{1,2\}). \tag{27)'$$

Applying strategy (2-2) prices remain constantly at the level $p_i{*}^c$, where index c denotes prices with respect to closed-loop control. This level $p_i{*}^c$ is given by

$$p_i{*}^c = \frac{c_i+(1+r)v_i}{1-(\varepsilon_j/D)} \; ; \qquad (i \in \{1,2\},\ i \neq j). \tag{19}'$$

I.e. in both cases, open-loop control and closed-loop control, prices are constant, if policy (2-2) applies. Possibly they are different; more precisely

$$p_i^* \leq p_i{*}^c \qquad (i \in \{1,2\}),$$

and equality holds, if one of the cross elasticities η_i vanishes. The properties of policies (1-3), (3-1), and (3-3) are equal to those of open-loop control.

In case of policy (2-3), where $\lambda_1 = v_1$ and $\ell_2 = (1/v_2)(p_2-c_2)x_2$ hold, one derives, applying equations (25) and (26)

$$\mu_1 = \frac{(1-(\varepsilon_2/D))(p_1{*}-p_1)}{\partial\ell_2/\partial x_2} \tag{28}$$

and

$$\dot{\mu}_1 = -\frac{\partial p_1}{\partial x_2}x_1 + ((1+r) - \frac{\partial\ell_2}{\partial x_2})\mu_1. \tag{29}$$

Differentiating (28) with respect to time and inserting this derivative into (29) one obtains by rearrangement

$$\pi_1(p_1+(\varepsilon_1+\eta_2)(p_1{*}-p_1)) + \pi_2(1-\eta_1-\varepsilon_2)(p_1{*}-p_1) = \\ = \frac{(p_2{*}-p_2)(p_1{*}-p_1)(1-(\varepsilon_1/D))(1-(\varepsilon_2/D))-(\eta_1\eta_2/D^2)p_1p_2}{v_2(1-(\varepsilon_2/D))}. \tag{30}$$

For the second player, who pursues maximal exploratory effort, one derives

$$-\varepsilon_2\pi_2 + \eta_2\pi_1 = (1/v_2)(p_2-\tilde{p}_2), \tag{31}$$

and, moreover,

$$p_1{*} = p_1{*}^c \text{ and } p_2{*} = p_2{*}^c \text{ hold.}$$

Now the price patterns p_1 and p_2 can be derived by equations (30) and (31), and they differ from those ones, obtained by open-loop control. Furthermore, the constant price $p_1 = p_1^*$ can be a solution of (30), only if η_1 or η_2 vanishes. Only in this case the open-loop solution coincides with the closed-loop solution. If policy (2-3) applies, neither the price nor the extraction rate of player 1 are constant. In order to discuss the strategies of the duopolists along a closed-loop equilibrium we once again make the assumptions (A1) - (A3) as well as the assumption

(A4) The cross elasticities η_1 and η_2 are equal.

Then there are the following Nash equilibria trajectories (see above p. 98):

s_1^c: (3-3) → (2-3) → (2-2)
s_2^c: (1-3) → (2-3) → (2-2)

Once again the phase space is divided by curve (23) into two parts and equivalently as above in case of open-loop control we only discuss one of the symmetric cases, i.e. player 1 can reach price p_1^{*c} by applying his policy 3, before player 2 can reach price p_2^{*c}.

Again two cases are to be distinguished:

a) (Maximal exploratory effort of both players).
Both players pursue maximal exploratory effort. Player 1 can apply policy 2 from time t_1^* on, while player 2 can apply policy 2 not before time t^* is reached, with $t_1^* < t^*$.

b) (Maximal exploratory effort only by the second player).
The second player only pursues initially maximal exploratory effort. Hence p_2 decreases, while p_1 increases, until time t_1^* is reached. From then on player 1 can apply policy 2. From then on regime (2-3) applies up to time t^*, from when on both players can apply policy 2, i.e. regime (2-2) is reached.

After time T, when no longer exploration can take place, the game collapses into the case of open-loop control.

IV.3 A Duopoly Model with Quantity Strategies

IV.3.1 Introduction of the Model.

Two suppliers of a finite nonrenewable exhaustible resource are determining the quantities of the resource to be supplied in order to maximize their discounted profits over a fixed time horizon. The price of the resource is given by the solution of the following differential equation:

$$\begin{aligned} \dot{p}(t) &= G(h(q(t)-p(t))) =: G(u)\,, \qquad t \in [0,T] \\ p(0) &= p^0. \end{aligned} \tag{32}$$

Obviously this price-demand structure is no longer as special as that one given by equation (7)′ in IV.2.

The planning horizon is given by time T; $q(t) := q_1(t) + q_2(t)$ denotes the amount of the resource supplied at time t, and G(u) denotes a monotonically increasing function satisfying

$$G(0) = 0\,, \quad G'(u) > 0 \quad \text{for all } u \in R.$$

This function G can be interpreted as speed of adjustment: Let $u = h(q(t_1)-p(t_1)) \neq 0$ at a certain point of time t_1, then the market price moves in the direction given by equation (32) until the equilibrium condition $h(q(t)-p(t)) = 0$ holds. Furthermore, the demand function, given implicitly by equation (32), has the property that increasing (decreasing) supply decreases (increases) price.
More precisely:
Using the notation

$$q(t) = \hat{q}(t)+\delta q(t)\,, \quad \delta q(t)>0 \quad t\in[0,T],$$

for all points (p,q), which satisfy (32) and satisfy $\frac{\partial f}{\partial q} < 0$, we have

$$p(t) = \hat{p}(t) + \delta p(t) + \text{"terms of higher order"}, \; \delta p(t)<0, \; t\in[0,T].$$

For this price adjustment process just described the supply rates $q_1(t)$ and $q_2(t)$ are the decision variables of the duopolists.
Let us further assume that the extraction costs per unit, $c_i(q_i(t))$, are convex with respect to q_i $(i \in \{1,2\})$.
The discounted profit of duopolist i is given by

$$J_i(q_1,q_2) = \int_0^T [p(t)q_i(t)-c_i(q_i(t))]e^{-rt}dt \ , \quad i\in\{1,2\}. \tag{33}$$

The constraints of the control variables are given by

$$0 \leq q_i \leq Q_i \text{ with } Q_i \leq x_i^0 \quad (i \in \{1,2\}). \tag{34}$$

By suitable choice of Q_i (34) is equivalent to

$$0 \leq \int_0^T q_i(t)dt \leq x_i^0 \ , \tag{34'}$$

where x_i^0 once again denotes the initial resource endowment of duopolist i.
The Hamiltonians of the related optimization problem are given by

$$\begin{aligned} H_i = {} & p(t)q_i(t,p(t))-c_i(q_i(t,p(t)) + \\ & + \lambda_i(t)f(p(t),q_1(t(p(t))+q_2(t,p(t))). \end{aligned} \quad (i\in\{1,2\})$$

Then a Nash equilibrium point (q_1^*,q_2^*) satisfies necessarily the subsequent conditions:

$$\begin{aligned} \dot{p}(t) &= f(p(t),q_1(t,p(t))+q_2(t,p(t))) \\ p(0) &= p^0 \\ \dot{\lambda}_i(t) &= \lambda_i(t)(r - \frac{\partial f}{\partial p} - \frac{\partial f}{\partial q_2}\frac{\partial q_2}{\partial q}) - q_i(t,p(t)) \\ H_i(t,p,q_i^*,q_j^*,\lambda_i) &= \max_{q_i} H_i(t,p,q_i,q_j^*,\lambda_i) \quad (i\in\{1,2\};\ i\neq j) \end{aligned} \tag{35}$$

with the boundary conditions

$$\lambda_i(T) = 0 \qquad (i \in \{1,2\}).$$

The discount factors are eliminated by a suitable choice of the multipliers λ_i.

Equations (35) and (34) yield

$$p(t) - \frac{dc_i}{dq_i} + \lambda_i(t)\frac{\partial f}{\partial q_i} \begin{cases} = 0 \text{ for } 0 < q_i(t,p(t)) < Q_i \\ < 0 \text{ for } q_i(t,p(t)) = 0 \\ > 0 \text{ for } q_i(t,p(t)) = Q_i \end{cases} \quad (36)$$

$(i \in \{1,2\})$.

Hence there exist nine policy regimes, out of which optimal extraction paths can be formed, i.e. depending on whether a duopolist does not at all exploit his reserves, whether he exploits as much as possible (bang-bang controls), or whether he chooses his extraction rate between those extremals.

IV.3.2 Specialization of the Model: Linear-Quadratic Differential Game

Since it seems to be hopeless to solve analytically the partial differential equations (35) and (36) simultaneously, we will discuss the following special case of a linear-quadratic differential game. Let us assume the differential equation (32) to be linear:

$$\dot{p}(t) = c - ap(t) - b(q_1(t)+q_2(t)), \quad a,b,c > 0, \quad (32)'$$

and the cost functions to be quadratic

$$c_i(q_i(t)) = \frac{1}{2}\alpha_i q_i^2(t), \quad (i \in \{1,2\};\ \alpha_i > 0). \quad (37)$$

Then profits (33) can be written:

$$J_i(q_1,q_2) = \int_0^T \left[p(t)q_i(t) - \frac{1}{2}\alpha_i q_i^2(t)\right] e^{-rt}dt \quad (i\in\{1,2\}) \quad (33)'$$

Furthermore, it has to be assumed:

$$Q_1 + Q_2 < a/b$$

in order to avoid negative prices.
Defining $s(t) := (c/a)-p(t)$, the demand relation (32)′ yields

$$\dot{s}(t) > -as(t)$$

and hence $s(t) > 0$ and $p(t) < c/a$ for all t. Thus the feasible region is a triangle in the p-q-plane, which is defined by the inequalities $0 < p < c/a$ and $0 < q < c/b$.
Combining results, we have

$$\dot{\lambda}_i(t) = (r+a+b\frac{\partial q_i(t,p(t))}{\partial p})\lambda_i(t)-q_i(t,p(t))-q_j(t,p(t)) \qquad (35)'$$

$$(i\varepsilon\{1,2\};\ i\neq j)$$

and

$$p(t)-\alpha_i q_i(t,p(t))-b\lambda_i(t) \quad \begin{cases} = 0, & 0 < q_i < Q_i \quad (a) \\ < 0, & q_i = 0 \quad (b) \\ > 0, & q_i = Q_i \quad (c) \end{cases} \qquad (36)'$$

$$(i\ \varepsilon\ \{1,2\}),$$

where $\lambda_1(T) = \lambda_2(T) = 0$ holds.

Now we can discuss the nine policy regimes of the Nash equilibria:

1. No extraction at all:
   For both duopolists equation (36)'(b) applies, i.e. $q_i^* = 0$ $(i\varepsilon\{1,2\})$, hence $p(t) < b\lambda_i$. However, considering $\lambda_i = \partial V_i/\partial p$ (see Starr and Ho, 1969a), where

   $$V_i = \int_t^T [p(\tau)q(\tau) - \frac{1}{2}\alpha_i q_i^2(\tau)]e^{-r\tau}d\tau,$$

   it can be seen that the price p is smaller than marginal revenue $b(\partial V_i/\partial p)$ for both duopolists. Hence it is best for both duopolists not to extract at all. However, this implies that the price rises, since $\dot{p}(t) = c - ap(t)$ holds.

2. No extraction by the first duopolist, extraction by the second one:
   Equation (36)'(a) applies for the second duopolist and inequality (36)'(b) applies for the first duopolist; i.e. $q_1^*(t,p(t)) = 0$ and $q_2^*(t,p(t)) > 0$. Hence $p(t) < b(\partial V_1/\partial p)$ and $p(t) > b(\partial V_2/\partial p)$.
   It is profitable to supply only for the second duopolist. I.e the second duopolist actually behaves as a monopolist, hence the models of Chapter I are applicable.

3. No extraction by the first duopolist, maximal extraction by the second one:
(36)'(b) applies for the first and (36)'(c) applies for the second duopolist; i.e. $q_1^* = 0$ and $q_2^* = Q_2$ hold. This regime differs from the second one only for the second duopolist: He acts as a monopolist and keeps the price low enough so that the potential competitor is kept out of the market.

4. Extraction below capacity by the first duopolist, maximal extraction by the second one:
(36)'(a) applies for the first and (36)'(c) applies for the second duopolist; i.e. $q_1^*(t,p(t)) > 0$ and $q_2^*(t,p(t)) = Q_2$ hold. Hence $p(t) > b(\partial V_i/\partial p)$ holds for both duopolists. The price, however, is high enough for the second duopolist, too. The first duopolist satisfies the remaining demand. He is able to act "monopolistically optimal", since he can rely on a no-change of the supply by the competitor.
The price of the resource is given by the differential equation

$$\dot{p}(t) = c - bQ_2 - ap(t) - bq_1(t).$$

5. Maximal extraction by both duopolists:
Inequality (36)'(c) applies for both duopolists. The market is divided into two separate markets.

6. Extraction by both duopolists below capacity:
(36)'(a) applies for both duopolists; this is the "real" duopoly situation. Hence we distinguish closed-loop and open-loop equilibria.

6.a) Closed-loop Equilibria:
The solutions of the boundary value problem (35)' are affin-linear extraction rates (=supply curves) of the form

$$q_i^*(t,p(t)) = \frac{1}{\alpha_i}(1-bk_i(t))p(t) - \frac{b}{\alpha_i}E_i(t) \quad (i\varepsilon\{1,2\}).$$

The functions $k_i(t)$ and $E_i(t)$ solve the differential equations

$$\dot{k}_i(t) = (r+2a+\frac{b}{\alpha_i}(1-bk_i)+2\frac{b}{\alpha_j}(1-bk_j))k_i - \frac{1}{\alpha_i}(1-bk_i) \tag{38}$$

and

$$\dot{E}_i(t) = (r+a+\frac{b}{\alpha_i}(1-bk_i)+\frac{b}{\alpha_j}(1-bk_j))E_i - \frac{b^2}{\alpha_j}k_iE_j-k_ic \tag{39}$$

for $i,j \in \{1,2\}$; $i \neq j$.

Equations (38) are of Riccati type and (39) are linear and can be solved in sequence to the solutions of (38).
Assuming this duopoly situation to apply during the interval $[t_1,t_2] \subseteq [0,T]$, the boundary conditions for (38) and (39) are given by

$$\lambda_i(t_2) = \frac{\partial V_i}{\partial p}\Big|_{t=t_2} \qquad (i\in \{1,2\}) \tag{40}$$

where $\lambda_i(t)$ can be determined as follows:

$$\lambda_i(t) = k_i(t)p(t) + E_i(t). \tag{41}$$

Since the value functions $V_i(t,p,q_1,q_2)$ are quadratic with respect to $p(t)$, the boundary conditions $k_i(t_2)$ and $E_i(t_2)$ can be obtained by the equations (40) and (41).

6.b) Open-loop Equilibria:
In addition to the extraction rates, which do depend on both, time <u>and</u> price, there exist solutions of the boundary value problem (35)' depending on time only. All partial derivatives $\partial q_i/\partial p$ in (35)' vanish and a solution is given directly in solving the respective system of ordinary differential equations. Since such systems can generally only be treated with qualitative methods, one can choose the following approach, where the system is transformed into a one-point boundary value problem. We assume that the multipliers $\lambda_i(t)$ of the open-loop problem are different from those ones in the closed-loop case and can be written as follows:

$$\lambda_i(t) = D_i(t)p_i(t) + F_i(t).$$

D_i and F_i denote the solutions of the following differential equations:

$$\dot{D}_i(t) = (r+2a+\frac{b}{\alpha_i}(1-bD_i)+\frac{b}{\alpha_j}(1-bD_j))D_i - \frac{1}{\alpha_i}(1-bD_i),$$

and

$$\dot{F}_i(t) = (r+a+\frac{b}{\alpha_i}(1-bD_i))F_i - \frac{b^2}{\alpha_j}D_iF_j - D_ic$$

for $i,j \in \{1,2\}$ and $i \neq j$.
By equation (36)'(a) we have

$$\dot{p}(t) = (a + \frac{b}{\alpha_1}(1-bD_1) + \frac{b}{\alpha_2}(1-bD_2))p(t) + c + \frac{b^2}{\alpha_1}F_1 + \frac{b^2}{\alpha_2}F_2 \tag{42}$$

$$=: \sigma(t)p(t) + \rho(t).$$

The solution of this differential equation gives the equilibrium path of the price due to open-loop control:

$$p^*(t) = p(t_1)e^{\int_{t_1}^{t}\sigma(\tau)d\tau} + \int_{t_1}^{t} e^{-\int_{t}^{t}\sigma(\beta)d\beta}\rho(\tau)d\tau.$$

Using this equilibrium price one obtains the optimal extraction rates by (36)'(a):

$$q_i^*(t) = \frac{1}{\alpha_i}(1-bD_i(t))\cdot$$

$$\cdot\left[p(t_1)e^{-\int_{t_1}^{t}\sigma(\tau)d\tau} + \int_{t_1}^{t} e^{-\int_{\tau}^{t}\sigma(\beta)d\beta}\rho(\tau)d\tau\right] - \frac{b}{\alpha_i}F_i(t).$$

These equilibria do not need to be the only ones. The conditions, as satisfied by these solutions, are only necessary conditions. So it is possible that combinations of open-loop and closed-loop Nash paths are equilibrium points, too.
The equilibria 7. - 9. are mirror images of 2. - 4.; one only has to reverse the numbering of the two duopolists.

The problem of ultimate exhaustion of the resource cannot be answered by this model, since it was assumed that even in case of maximal extraction the resource cannot be exhausted during the finite time period $[0,T]$ due to capacity constraints (34).

IV.4 Cartelization and Optimal Extraction of Exhaustible Resources

Another topic of interest in the theory of optimal extraction of exhaustible resources is the role of cartelization.
This section will discuss a model of Ulph and Folie (1980), where this problem is treated. Specifically we will discuss the effects, due to those resource suppliers, who do not participate at the cartel. One illustration may be OPEC and its implications to oil extracting countries outside e.g. the US, the United Kingdom, or Norway. There is a widespread belief that these countries can also profit by the partial cartelization of the market (see e.g. Salant, 1976). However, it will be shown that this depends decisively on the cost structure.
We assume that the suppliers, not participating at the cartel, act as in pure competition. I.e. they are compelled to take the price of the resource, set by the cartel, as given. However, the cartel has to consider the quantities, sold by the outside suppliers.
The terms of interest related to members of the cartel, are denoted by the index 1, and those to outside suppliers by the index 2.
Moreover, two cases will be distinguished: Both sides behave competitively (pure competition), or the cartel behaves monopolistically (monopolistic behaviour).

IV.4.1 Pure Competition

We assume that all members of the cartel are facing identical constant marginal extraction costs c_1, and all suppliers, who are not members of the cartel and who will be called the "non-cartel", are facing identical constant marginal extraction costs c_2.
We further assume that demand is linear

$$p(t) = A - aq_1(t) - aq_2(t) \; ; \quad A,a > 0 \; , \quad A > \max(c_1,c_2) \qquad (1)'$$

where A denotes the price, at which the demand of the resource vanishes.

All decision makers use quantity strategies, hence they are looking for extraction paths so as to maximize the present value of their profits subject to the usual constraint that they cannot supply more than their initial resource endowment. This objective will equalize discounted profits for all time intervals of actual resource extraction. In periods without extraction discounted profit can only be lower. Otherwise discounted profit could be enlarged by changing the extraction policy without violating the constraints. Denoting the maximal present marginal profit of the cartel and the non-cartel by ρ_1 and ρ_2, respectively, and the price path subject to pure competition by $\pi(t)$, one obtains the following equilibrium conditions:

$$\pi(t) \leqslant c_i+\rho_i e^{rt}, \quad q_i(t) \geqslant 0 \quad (i\varepsilon\{1,2\}).$$

Due to the assumption of constant marginal extraction costs, there can be resource extraction only by either the cartel or the non-cartel. The supplier facing the lower costs will deplete his reserves first, and only after the other will start supplying. Hence assuming that the marginal costs of the cartel are lower (without restricting generality), $c_1 < c_2$, in case of pure competition the model is characterized by two consecutive intervals:

$$\text{(i)} \quad 0 \leqslant t \leqslant \sigma: \pi(t) = c_1+\rho_1 e^{rt}, \quad q1(t) > 0, \; q2(t) = 0,$$

$$\text{(ii)} \quad \sigma \leqslant t \leqslant T: \pi(t) = c2+\rho 2e^{rt}, \quad q1(t) = 0, \; q2(t) > 0.$$

The values ρ_1 and $\rho 2$ can be interpreted as rents of resource extraction. These rents are the only possibility to make profit in case of pure competition. The present value of these rents, i.e. the profits of e.g. the non-cartel are given by

$$\int_\sigma^T \rho_2 e^{rt} q_2(t) e^{-rt} dt = \rho_2 \int_\sigma^T q_2(t) dt = \rho_2 x_2(0).$$

IV.4.2 Monopolistic Behaviour of the Cartel

We will analyze the behaviour of both groups for the case that the cartel behaves monopolistically, yet will be restricted by the non-cartel. More precisely, it is assumed that the cartel follows the rules of a noncooperative Nash game. The non-cartel adopts the cartel price and chooses an extraction path $q_2(t)$ such that its discounted profit becomes maximal. Hence the equilibrium condition is once again given by

$$p(t) \leq c_2+R_2e^{rt} \;, \quad q_2(t) \geq 0 \;, \tag{43}$$

where p(t) denotes the equilibrium price of the Nash game and R_2 denotes the rents of the non-cartel.
The cartel takes the extraction policies of the non-cartel as given and determines an extraction path $q_1(t)$, which maximizes discounted profits subject to the usual resource constraints. I.e. the cartel subtracts the extraction rate of the non-cartel from total demand and satisfies the remaining demand.
Then marginal revenue of the cartel is given by $p(t) - aq_1(t)$ and consequently marginal profit by $p(t) - aq_1(t) - c_1$.
The equilibrium condition for the cartel is given by:

$$p(t) - aq_1(t) \leq c_1 + R_1e^{rt} \;, \quad q_1(t) \geq 0 \;. \tag{44}$$

The notations are analogous to the case of the non-cartel.
In order to derive a market equilibrium, the actual extraction path of non-cartel, has to coincide with the one as considered by cartel. The price development as conjectured by the non-cartel, has to agree with the actual price decision of the cartel. Moreover, these decisions have to agree with the market conditions.
Precisely, $q_i(t)$ and p(t) have to satisfy the conditions (1), (43), and (44).
Up to the point of time, when all reserves are used up, three cases have to be distinguished depending whether the cartel or the non-cartel or both extract simultaneously:

1. Cartel extraction only:
   By the conditions (1), (43), and (44) one obtains the market price

$$p(t) = A-aq_1(t) = c_1 + aq_1(t) + R_1e^{rt} < c_2 + R_2e^{rt}.$$

   Considering $q_1(t) > 0$ in (44) we have

$$c_1+R_1e^{rt} < p(t) = \frac{1}{2}(A+c_1)+\frac{1}{2}R_1e^{rt} < c_2+R_2e^{rt}.$$

   Hence one derives the following conditions:

$$p(t) = \frac{1}{2}(A+c_1) + \frac{1}{2}R_1e^{rt}$$

   and

$$c_1 + R_1e^{rt} < \frac{1}{2}(A+c_1) + \frac{1}{2}R_1e^{rt} < c_2 + R_2e^{rt}.$$

2. Non-cartel extraction only:
   Considering $q_1(t) = 0$ in (44) one derives by (1), (43), and (44)

$$p(t) = c_2 + R_2e^{rt}$$

   and

$$c_2 + R_2e^{rt} < c_1 + R_1e^{rt} < \frac{1}{2}(A+c_1) + \frac{1}{2}R_1e^{rt}.$$

3. Simultaneous extraction:
   Since $q_i > 0$ $(i\varepsilon\{1,2\})$, one derives from (1), (43), and (44) the subsequent equilibrium conditions, which only depend on the costs and rents of the cartel:

$$p(t) = c_2 + R_2e^{rt} < c_1 + R_1e^{rt} < \frac{1}{2}(A+c_1) + \frac{1}{2}R_1e^{rt}.$$

In particular, in equilibrium each of both groups, extract until ultimate exhaustion of the respective reserves.

Suppose, the cartel extracts during a period before the time t*, then - independent on whether the non-cartel does or does not extract -

$$c_1 + R_1e^{rt} < c_2 + R_2e^{rt}$$

will apply with equality at time t*.
If at this point of time only the members of the non-cartel will extract, then from then on

$$c_2 + R_2e^{rt} < c_1 + R_1e^{rt}$$

will apply and once again it will apply with equality at time t*.
However, since these two price curves can cross only once, i.e at time t*, there cannot exist another period, during which the cartel extracts again.
A second implication of the equilibrium conditions is the impossibility of a period with extraction by one group only following directly to a period with extraction by the other group. Suppose, until time t* only the cartel extracts, and from then on only the non-cartel extracts, then

$$c_1 + R_1e^{rt^*} < c_2 + R_2e^{rt^*}$$

and

$$c_1 + R_1e^{rt^*} > c_2 + R_2e^{rt^*}.$$

must apply simultaneously.
Hence there has to be a period of simultaneous extraction between these two periods.
Finally, if ultimate exhaustion of the resource will happen during a period of simultaneous extraction, there cannot have been a period of single group extraction before.
Suppose, at time T, when

$$c_1+R_1 = \frac{1}{2}(A+c_1) + \frac{1}{2}R_1e^{rT} = A$$

applies, will be later than t*, then before time T the inequality

$$c_1+R_1 < \frac{1}{2}(A+c_1) + \frac{1}{2}R_1e^{rt} < c_2 + R_2e^{rt},$$

must apply and that means that only the cartel extracts its reserves. Only for $t^* = T$ each of the three curves can cross in this and only in this point. Hence the relation of the three possible price levels, which applies just before time $t^* = T$, must also hold for all $t < T$ and that means that both groups extract simultaneously.

IV.4.3 Implications of Cartelization to the Profits of the Non-Cartel

Assuming constant marginal costs the discounted profit of the non-cartel in case of pure competition is given by $\rho_2 x_2(0)$ (see 4.1). Accordingly in the Nash model it has the value $R_2 x_2(0)$. In order to show that the profits of the non-cartel decrease, if the cartel behaves monopolistic, it is sufficient to show $R_2 < \rho_2$.
As mentioned in IV.4.1 we assume that $(1/2)(A+c_1) < c_2$; i.e. the members of the cartel are facing a better cost structure. This could be just the reason why the cartel is built. In this case there are only two different equilibrium price paths in the Nash model:

Case 1: Two price regimes
Initially only the cartel exploits its reserves, until at a certain point of time the members of the non-cartel begin to extract, too. From then on simultaneous extraction takes place until time S, when ultimate exhaustion of the cartel's reserves will be reached. From then on only the non-cartel will extract until ultimate exhaustion of its reserves will be reached, too.
The price development is then given by the two equations

$$p(t) = \frac{1}{2}(A+c_1) + \frac{1}{2}R_1 e^{rt}, \qquad 0 \leq t \leq S$$

and

$$p(t) = c_2 + R_2 e^{rt} \qquad , \qquad S \leq t \leq T.$$

This price path and that one in case of pure competition behave according to the following figure:

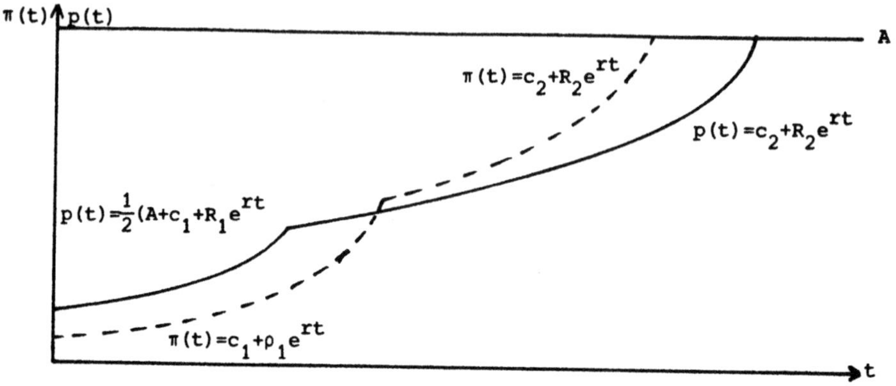

Only the development of this figure can occur. For proof suppose, this would not be so. Then, on the one hand, initially $p(t) < \pi(t)$ could hold, and that means that

$$\frac{1}{2}(A+c_1) + \frac{1}{2}R_1 < c_1 + \rho_1$$

holds.

Since

$$\frac{1}{2}(A + C_1) > c_1 ,$$

one also obtains

$$\frac{1}{2}R_1 < \rho_1$$

and hence the curve

$$\frac{1}{2}(A+c_1) + \frac{1}{2}R_1 e^{rt}$$

runs strictly below the curve

$$c_1 + \rho_1 e^{rt} \quad \text{for all } t > 0.$$

Hence the initial extraction rate of the cartel has to be greater than its extraction rate in case of pure competition. Since further both groups extract simultaneously their reserves, the change from the Nash curve to the competitive curve has to happen before time σ when the cartel is built. Otherwise the reserves of the cartel would be exhausted, before the non-cartel starts to extract.

However, this assumption yields that the price curve

$$c_2 + R_2e^{rt}$$

must run below the curve

$$c_2 + \rho_2e^{rt}.$$

However, this cannot happen, since otherwise the resource would be exhausted before the price level A would have been reached.
Hence initially the price curve

$$p(t) = \frac{1}{2}(A+c_1) + \frac{1}{2}R_1e^{rt}$$

runs above the curve

$$\pi(t) = c_1 + \rho_1e^{rt}.$$

However, the price development of the figure above, could be violated, if $R_2 > \rho_2$ holds. Then the extraction rate of non-cartel during the a period (σ,τ) after the cartel is built, could not exceed the competitive extraction rate. And since the cartel also extracts, if the price is given by $c_2 + R_2e^{rt}$, the point of intersection of the two curves

$$c_2+R_2e^{rt}$$

and

$$\frac{1}{2}(A + c_1 + R_1e^{rt})$$

can be before time σ.
Yet this implies that price p(t) always has to be at least as high as $\pi(t)$ and during some time intervals it has to be strictly higher.
However, such prices can only occur, if in the Nash model the price $p(t) = A$ will be reached before all reserves will have been exhausted.
Consequently $\rho_2 > R_2$ must apply.

Case 2: One price regime

The price development is given by the following figure:

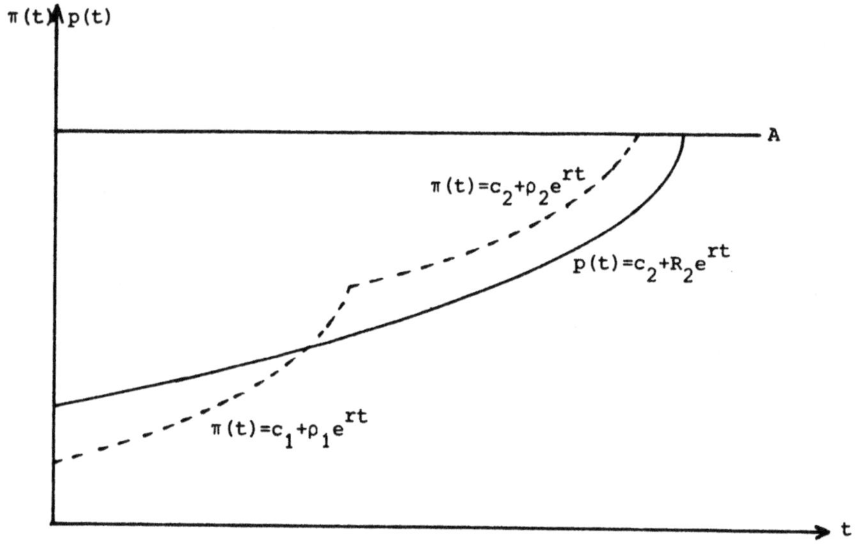

Suppose, $R_2 > \rho_2$, then the price curve of the Nash model would run on or above the higher branch of the competitive price path. However, this would affect that the price would reach the value A before all reserves would be exhausted. Consequently in this case $\rho_2 > R_2$ must hold, too.

Summarizing, provided that the cartel faces a significant cost advantage, the discounted profits of the members of the non-cartel decrease even further by cartelization.

IV.5 Oligopoly with Discrete Time Parameter

All models discussed so far are restricted to two players. On the one hand one can indeed obtain typical solution approaches and results for oligopolistic markets, but on the other hand in particular the results can differ significantly from those ones obtainable in games with three or more players.

Since the analytical solution of the systems of differential equations of N-person differential games (N > 2) becomes more and more difficult or even impossible, we now turn over to numerical determination of the Nash equilibria. Consequently one has to realize that there can be made conclusions to the nature of solutions by means of examples only. On the other hand there is the advantage to analyze games with different structures without great expenditure, and particularly those ones, which cannot be analyzed analytically at all. These two aspects - more than two players and numerical determination of Nash points - do motivate the discussion of the following model. Even though the formulation is discrete, and the model of chapter V is continuous like the previous models, this section will serve for preparation of the algorithmic results of the final chapter.

This model is developped by Salant (1982).

The notation used below differs from the one used until now in that index t denotes the respective period under consideration.

The problem is given by the determination of extraction paths q_i^t, which, together with the corresponding price path p_t, maximize the objective function

$$\sum_{t=1}^{T} \beta^{t-1}(p^t q_i^t - c_i^t(q_i^t)) \quad (i=1,2,\dots,N) \tag{45}$$

of each of the N oligopolists, subject to the constraints

$$0 \leq q_i^t \leq Q_i^t \text{ (given)}, \quad (t=1,2,\dots,T)$$

$$\sum_{t=1}^{T} q_i^t \leq x_i^0 \qquad (i=1,2,\dots,N). \tag{46}$$

Here β denotes the discount factor corresponding to the discount rate r.

Further it will be distinguished between suppliers, who behave competitively, and those, who behave as Nash players (see IV.4).

The price of the resource is given by the equation

$$\sum_{i=1}^{N} q_i^{\,t} = D_t(p^t), \tag{47}$$

i.e. D_t denotes the demand during period t (t = 1,2,...,T).
In the following the (necessary) Kuhn-Tucker conditions of the optimization problem (45) and (46) are listed. For the sake of clarity we restrict ourselves to two players, the first of them behaving as competitor, the second one as Nash player. The conditions obtained can be generalized to more than two players straightforward.
For the solution of the maximization problem of the first supplier one derives the following Lagrange function

$$L(q^t,\alpha^t,\lambda^t) = \sum_{t=1}^{T} \beta^{t-1}(p^t q^t - c^t(q^t)) + \alpha^t(Q^t - q^t) + \lambda(x_o - \sum_{t=1}^{T} q_t). \tag{48}$$

The Kuhn-Tucker conditions for an optimal extraction program are then given as follows

1. a) $q_1^t > 0$ for all t

   b) $L_{q_1^t} < 0$, where $L_{q_1^t} = \beta^{t-1}(p^t - c_1'^{\,t}(q_1^t)) - \alpha_1^t - \lambda_1$ (49)

   c) $q_1^t L_{q_1^t} = 0$ for all t = 1,2,...,T.

2. a) $\alpha_1^t > 0$

   b) $L_{\alpha_1^t} > 0$, where $L_{\alpha_1^t} = Q_1^t - q_1^t$ (50)

   c) $\alpha_1^t L_{\alpha_1^t} = 0$ for all t = 1,2,...,T.

3. a) $\lambda_1 > 0$

   b) $L_{\lambda_1} > 0$, where $L_{\lambda_1} = x_1^o - \sum_{t=1}^{T} q_1$ (51)

   c) $\lambda_1 L_{\lambda_1} = 0.$

In case of strictly convex cost functions the objective function of the first supplier is strictly concave, too, and if the feasible control set is convex, then, given a price sequence p^t, there exists exactly one solution $(q_1^{\,1},\dots,q_1^{\,T})$.
For the solution of the other player, the Nash player, one derives the following Lagrange function:

$$L(q_2^1,\dots,q_2^T;\alpha_2^1,\dots,\alpha_2^T;\lambda_2;p^1,\dots,p^T;\gamma_2^1,\dots,\gamma_2^T) =$$

$$= \sum_{t=1}^{T} (\beta^{t-1}(p^t q_2^t - c_2^t(q_2^t)) + \alpha_2^t(Q_2^t - q_2^t) + \gamma_2^t(D_t(p^t) - q_1^t - q_2^t)) + \lambda_2(x_2^o - \sum_{t=1}^{T} q_2^t)$$

This function is different from the Lagrange function (48), since the Nash player supplies at each time exactly the difference between total demand and the supply rate of the competitor.
From this Lagrangean one derives the following necessary conditions for an optimal extraction program:

1. a) $q_2 \geq 0$

   b) $L_{q_2^t} \leq 0$, where $L_{q_2^t} = \beta^{t-1}(p^t - c'^t_2(q_2^t)) - \gamma_2^t - \lambda_2 - \alpha_2^t$ (52)

   c) $p_2 L_{q_2^t} = 0$ for all $t = 1,2,\dots,T$;

2. a) $\alpha_2^t \geq 0$

   b) $L_{\alpha_2^t} \geq 0$, where $L_{\alpha_2^t} = Q_2^t - q_2^t$ (53)

   c) $\alpha_2^t L_{\alpha_2^t} = 0$ for all $t = 1,2,\dots,T$;

3. a) $\lambda_2 \geq 0$

   b) $L_{\lambda_2} \geq 0$, where $L_{\lambda_2} = x_2^o - \sum_{t=1}^{T} q_2$ (54)

   c) $\lambda_2 L_{\lambda_2} = 0$;

4. a) $p^t \geq 0$

b) $L_{p^t} \leq 0$, where $L_{p^t} = \lambda_2^t D_t'(p^t) + \beta^{t-1} q_2^t$ (55)

c) $p^t L_{p^t} = 0$ for all $t = 1,2,\ldots,T$;

5. $L_{\lambda_2^t} = 0$, where $L_{\lambda_2^t} = D_t(p^t) - q_1^t - q_2^t$ for all $t = 1,2,\ldots,T$. (56)

Assuming the existence of the inverse demand function and inserting it into the objective function of the second supplier, one derives as sufficient condition for a solution of the second supplier's maximum problem being unique that the function

$$D_t^{-1}(q_1^t + q_2^t)q_2^t - c_2^t(q_2^t)$$

has to be strictly concave with respect to q_2^t.
The optimality conditions (49) - (51) and (52) - (56) can be realized simultaneously by applying the following algorithm:

<u>Step 1:</u> (Initialization). Choose initial values of the multiplier λ subject to both suppliers.

<u>Step 2:</u> (Main step). $t = 1$.

a) Choose a positive price p^t.

b) Determine the corresponding extraction rates by the conditions 1. and 2.

c) Check by (56), whether the extraction policies agree with the respective demand.
In case of failure improve p^t according to the sign of the deviation between demand and supply and return to b).
Otherwise set $t = t+1$ and go to step 3, if $t > T$, else go to step 2.a).

<u>Step 3:</u> (Feasibility check). Check, whether the cumulative quantitities supplied, exceed the respective initial amounts x_o^i.
If the transversality conditions are violated in one case, change the respective multipliers according to the sign of the deviation and return to 2.a).
Else, stop.

A survey of this algorithm is given by the subsequent flow diagram of one iteration of steps 2 and 3:

Choose the multipliers $\lambda_1{}^t$ and $\lambda_2{}^t$.

↓

Set the market price $p := p^t > 0$.

↓

Determine the extraction rates q_i by (49) and (52) with $\alpha^i=0$.

↓

Prove the feasibility of the extraction rates:

If $q^i<0$, set $q^i=0$,

if $q^i>Q^i$, set $q^i=Q^i$.

↓

Determine the multipliers α_1 by (50).

↓

Determine the multipliers γ_2 by (52).

↓

Determine the multipliers α_2 by (53).

↓

Prove the market being in equilibrium by (56):

If $L_{\lambda_2}>0$, set $p=p_o+\delta$,

if $L_{\lambda_2}<0$, set $p=p_o-\delta$,

if $L_{\lambda_2}=0$, continue.

↓

New period $t = t+1$:

If $t < T$, set $t := t+1$

if $t > T$, continue.

↓

Prove the transversality conditions:

If $\Sigma q_t > x_o$,

if $\Sigma q_t < x_o$

↓

End.

The existence of those equilibria can be assured by the usual assumptions (concavity of the objective functions). Those assumptions are related to the properties of the cost and demand functions. In case of e.g. linear demand an equilibrium is even uniquely determined.
Within this basic structure various properties of the model can be analyzed. For illustration we present some possible extensions.
One can e.g. think of depletion effects in the sense that there are qualitative differences between different plants of the resource. Those effects can be incorporated in the model by treating the resource, which can be extracted at a particular marginal cost, as the reserve of a separate plant.
Another topic, which can be incorporated in the model, is the problem of perfect substitution of the resource by another commodity. E.g. oil produced from liquified coal can be assumed to be identical with natural oil. Consequently both kinds of oil are sold at the same price. Considering the cost structure of the oil produced from liquified coal, however, there are problems. One has not only to consider the state of technology with regard to the liquification of the coal, but also the price of the coal. This price can assumed to be exogenously given or can be determined endogenously in the model. The latter seems to be much more realistic, since the liquification of coal only makes sense, when the price of natural oil is increased so far that the production of liquified coal is profitable. But on the other hand the employment of coal provides implications to extraction and price of the natural oil or of oil in general, too.

IV.6. Conclusions

The chapter dealt with oligopolistic models of resource extraction mainly with respect to analytic solutions of duopolies. The solution concept used has been the Nash equilibrium. The reason for the choice of this concept is given by the restriction to non-cooperative oligopolies.

The first model has been a simple illustrative model with bang-bang controls as solutions. All players were assumed to face identical cost and demand functions and consequently they all behave equal: the extraction rates decline exponentially. That means particularly that the resource will never be exhausted at all. The level of the respective extraction rates is given by the initial resource endowments of the oligopolists.

The next analyzed step was to distinguish between open-loop and closed-loop controls in case of a duopoly with price strategy on the one hand and with quantity strategy on the other hand.

In case of open-loop Nash price strategies the extraction rates depend mainly on the elasticity of demand with respect to the price. The equilibrium points are characterized by the fact that both duopolists reach a policy, where exploration of further deposits and simultaneous extraction by both duopolists occur.

In case of closed-loop Nash controls the equilibria are very similar: Finally, the prices of the resource, set by both duopolists, are equal, and exploration of further deposits and extraction of the resource occur simultaneously. However, the price level of open-loop and closed-loop control differ. Once again it depends mainly on the elasticity of demand with respect to price.

The open-loop price and the closed-loop price coincide only if the cross-elasticities of demand vanish.

In case of quantity strategies optimal policies are composed of different policy regimes, depending on whether they are bang-bang controls and whether both duopolists do or do not extract their reserves simultaneously. Obviously these regimes do depend on the cost and demand structure.

The next topic has been the problem of cartelization of a part of the resource market. The main result has been the forcing down of profits of the non-cartel members, provided the members of the cartel have cost advantages.

Finally for the open-loop Nash problem a model with discrete time parameter and with more than two players was introduced, and an algorithm for the numerical treatment of this model was described. Moreover, possible extensions of the basic model have been sketched. Main emphasis of the model has been to prepare for chapter V.

V. OLIGOPOLISTIC EXTRACTION WITH CONTINUOUS TIME

The chapter analyzes a model of an oligopolistic resource market with continuous time parameter. I.e. the time horizon T will not be divided into distinct periods, at the beginning of which the strategies of the players are to be chosen, but the strategies have to be fixed initially for the whole period up to T. This procedure represents the transition from discrete time to continuous time by reducing the length of the subperiods arbitrarily (see chapter III, Definition 1).

There is a nice motivation for this procedure, since there are - beyond all short-run fluctuations - long-run plans, which can be understood at least as projections of the decision makers.

The choice of the informational structure, i.e. whether open-loop or closed-loop controls should be used, depends on what necessary information for the determination of closed-loop controls is available in general. Rigorously this problem has to be analyzed by stochastic (differential) games.

However, we restrict ourselves to the discussion of deterministic models. Hence we will determine open-loop controls of the respective games. In addition it will be assumed that the strategies of the players can only consider changes of the state of the game, which are known initially.

Two types of games will be discussed: Ones with quantity strategies and ones with price strategies. The latter ones are of minor interest, since the resource will be treated as a homogeneous good and hence the solutions differ only, if capacity constraints cause the prices to differ.

V.1 Basic Model with Quantity Strategies

V.1.1 Introduction of the Model

Throughout this section the subsequent assumptions hold:

(A1) The resource is continuously extractable.

(A2) Only the extraction rate can be controlled.

(A3) The total resource stock is of finite size.

(A4) The price is determined by a given demand function.

(A5) The market is cleared at each instant of time.

(A6) The resource is a homogeneous good.

(A7) The extraction costs depend on the remaining amount of the resource.

The oligopolists are choosing extraction rates so as to maximize their discounted profits. The price depends on the flow of the resource, i.e. it depends on the total supply of the resource (A4). Suppose further a fixed planning horizon T. The extraction costs depend, according to (A7), on the amount $x(t)$ of the resource, available at time t, $t \in [0,T]$. The respective cost functions are assumed to be strictly monotonically decreasing and convex with respect to x, and twice differentiable:

$$c_i = c_i(x_i(t)) \ , \quad c_i'(x_i) < 0 \ , \quad c_i''(x_i) > 0. \tag{1}$$

Moreover, the extraction costs of the oligopolists do depend either on the remaining part of the resource stock of each oligopolist, or on the total resource stock.
In the first case each supplier owns some reserves, and it is implicitly assumed that he will exploit first those, which can be depleted at the lowest cost. (For a justification of this assumption see Kemp and Long, 1980b). In the second case all oligopolists are producers of a pool, and the extracted quantities by one oligopolist affect the extraction costs of all other ones. In this case obviously (A7) applies in the sense of conditions (1), too.

With the usual notations the price is given by the demand function (A4)

$$p = p(\sum_{i=1}^{N} q_i(t)) =: p(Q(t)), \tag{2}$$

where p is assumed to be strictly monotonically decreasing and concave with respect to Q.

Using further the cost functions (1) the maximization problem, which has to be solved simultaneously by all oligopolists, corresponds to a differential game with the following state equations

$$\begin{aligned} \dot{x}_i(t) &= -q_i(t) \qquad (i=1,2,\dots,N;\ t\in[0,T]) \\ x_i(0) &= x_i^0, \end{aligned} \tag{3}$$

where x_i^0 once again denotes the initial amount of the resource, available to player i.

The constraints related to the control variables $q_i(t)$ are given by

$$\int_0^T q_i(t)dt \leq x_i^0 \quad \text{for all} \quad i = 1,2,\dots,N \quad \text{and}$$

$$q_i(t) \geq 0 \quad \text{for} \quad t \in [0,T].$$

These conditions are equivalent with

$$0 \leq q_i \leq \bar{q}_i \;<=>:\; q_i \in Q_i \tag{4}$$

for suitable $\bar{q}_i$.

Hence the extracted resource quantity cannot exceed the respective initial amount of the resource.

The payoff functionals of the players are given by

$$\begin{aligned} J_i(q_1,\dots,q_N) &= g(x(T)) + \int_0^T q_i(t)e^{-r_i t}[p(\sum_{i=1}^{N} q_i(t))-c_i(x_i(t))]dt \\ &=: g(x(T)) + \int_0^T L^i(q,x;t)dt. \end{aligned} \tag{5}$$

Due to the assumption of g being concave in x, the convexity of the c_i and the concavity of the demand function (2) all J_i must be concave. By the concavity of the J_i's and the linearity of the state equations an open-loop Nash equilibrium point exists (see Scalzo, 1974).

The discount rates r_i can be different for the different oligopolists. The function $g(x(T))$, can be interpreted as the value of the terminal resource stock at time T, or as the exspected profit, gained by later extraction, respectively.
The Hamiltonians are

$$H_i = L^i(q,x;t) - \lambda_i(t)q_i(t) + \mu_i(t)\left[\int_0^T q_i(t)dt - x_i^0\right]. \qquad (6)$$

These functions have to be maximized for each player. The necessary conditions for a maximum of these functions are also necessary conditions for Nash equilibrium points, i.e. for controls $(q_1^*, q_2^*, \ldots, q_N^*)$ with

$$J_i(q_1^*, \ldots, q_{i-1}^*, q_i, q_{i+1}^*, \ldots, q_N^*) \leq J_i(q_1^*, \ldots, q_N^*) \qquad (7)$$

for all i=1,2,...,N (see chapter III, Definition 2).
I.e. a Nash equilibrium point maximizes all Hamiltonians.
If the cost functions are strictly convex and the demand function concave or - vice versa - the demand function is strictly concave and the cost functions are convex, these conditions are even sufficient. By this sharpening of the assumptions the Hamiltonians are strictly concave and there exists one unique maximum of each H_i, and this maximum corresponds to the unique Nash point.
The necessary conditions for the Hamiltonians H_i to be maximal are

$$\dot{\lambda}_i = L^i_{x_i} \qquad (i=1,2,\ldots,N) \qquad (8)$$

$$\lambda_i = -L^i_{q_i} \qquad (i=1,2,\ldots,N) \qquad (9)$$

$$\mu_i(t) = 0 \quad \text{or} \quad x_i^0 = \int_0^T q_i(t)dt \qquad (i=1,2,\ldots,N) \qquad (10)$$

Conditions (8) and (9) lead to the equation

$$-L^i_{x_i} = \frac{d}{dt}L^i_{q_i} \qquad (i=1,2,\ldots,N). \qquad (11)$$

V.1.2 Algorithm for the Determination of a Nash Equilibrium

In order to determine a Nash equilibrium point according to equations (3) - (5) numerically, a first order gradient algorithm is applied. The algorithm follows rather directly from the theory of section 1. It is actually implemented and extensively tested by a number of examples. Some of which are taken from the literature.
The algorithmic flow is straightforward: Starting from initial "solutions" $q_i(t)$, the algorithm approaches the equilibrium controls $q_i^*(t)$ iteratively; the equilibrium controls $q_i^*(t)$ satisfy the condition (see Bryson and Ho, 1975)

$$\frac{\partial H_i}{\partial q_i} = 0.$$

More precisely this algorithm is designed as follows:

1. Choose an initial solution $(q_1, \ldots, q_N)$.
2. Determine the corresponding state variables by the state equations.
3. Determine the values of the multipliers λ_i by equation (8).
4. Determine the values of $\partial H_i/\partial q_i$, which are in general different from zero.
5. Change the initial solutions by the values $\Delta q_i := W_i(\partial H_i/\partial q_i)$, where W_i are positive weights.
6. Repeat steps 1.-5. until the differences of the values of the respective payoff-functionals in two succeeding iterations are sufficiently small.

Schematically the algorithm is given by the subsequent flow diagram:

Choice of the initial solutions $q_i^{(1)}$ *).

↓

Determination of the size of the resource stocks $x_i^{(k)}$ by (3).

↓

Computation of the payoffs $J_i^{(k)}$.

↓

Stopping condition:

$|J_i^{(k)} - J_i^{(k-1)}| < \varepsilon \longrightarrow$ End.

$|J_i^{(k)} - J_i^{(k-1)}| > \varepsilon$ Continue.

↓

Determination of the multipliers $\lambda_i^{(k)}$ by (8).

↓

Determination of $\dfrac{\partial H_i^{(k)}}{\partial q_i^{(k)}}$ (equilibrium condition).

↓

Set $\Delta q_i = W_i\left(\dfrac{\partial H_i^{(k)}}{\partial q_i^{(k)}}\right)$ (Change of the extraction rates).

↓

Set $q_i^{(k+1)} = q_i^{(k)} + \Delta q_i$ (new extraction rates).

↓

Feasibility of the extraction rates

If $q_i^{(k+1)} \notin Q_i$ set $q_i^{(k+1)} = pr_{Q_i}(q_i^{(k+1)})$**). (→ return to determination of the resource stocks)

---

*) Numbers in bracketts denote the iteration index.

**) $pr_{Q_i}(\cdot)$ denotes the projection onto Q_i.

These steps are to be done simultaneously for each of the N players, whereby the respective controls of the players $i = 1,2,\ldots,N$ have impacts to the values of the payoff-functionals of all other players $j \neq i$, too.
The algorithm stops, when the values of the payoffs of each of the N players do not change significantly at two succeeding iterations.
Subsequently the algorithm will be introduced more precisely. The implementation is done for more than two players, but for clarity the description below is given for two players.
Further it is - without restricting generality - assumed that the control variables as well as the state variables are functions of the kind $f: [0,T] \to \mathbb{R}$; thus they are not vector-valued, although in general this is the case in optimal control problems. However, the algorithm introduced below can be directly extended along those lines.
In particular, the state variable is extended by the respective payoff functional and the new state variable is given by

$$\tilde{x}_i = \binom{x_i}{J_i}, \quad \tilde{x}^0 = \binom{x_i^0}{0}; \quad (i \in \{1,2\}).$$

Since for both players identical computations have to be done, in the following the index, denoting the player, will be omitted.
The state equations are of the form

$$\dot{\tilde{x}} = \tilde{f}(\tilde{x},q_1,q_2,t), \quad \tilde{x}(0) = \tilde{x}^0, \quad t \in [0,T]. \tag{3)'$$

with

$$\tilde{f} = \binom{f}{L}.$$

Now let q_1 and q_2 denote arbitrarily chosen controls and $\tilde{x}$ the corresponding trajectory, determined by the state equation (3)'. Let further Δq_1 and Δq_2 denote changes of the controls, such that the new controls $q_i+\Delta q_i$ $(i=1,2)$ generate the new trajectory $x+\Delta x$; then the state equation (3)' can be linearized as follows:

$$\Delta\dot{\tilde{x}} = \tilde{f}_{\tilde{x}}\Delta\tilde{x} + \tilde{f}_{q_1}\Delta q_1 + \tilde{f}_{q_2}\Delta q_2, \quad \Delta\tilde{x}(0)=0, \quad t\in[0,T]. \tag{12}$$

Now suppose, only the first player changes his control function, i.e. $\Delta q_2 = 0$, then a solution of (12) is given by

$$\Delta\tilde{x}_1\big|_T = \int_0^T \tilde{X}(t)\tilde{f}_{q_1}\Delta q_1(t)dt,$$

where the (2×2)-matrix $\tilde{X}(t)$ satisfies the following differential equation:

$$\dot{\tilde{X}} = \tilde{X}\tilde{f}_{\tilde{x}}\ , \quad \tilde{X}(T) = I\ , \quad t \in [0,T]. \tag{13}$$

The change of the first player's payoff is then given by

$$\Delta\tilde{J}_1 = \int_0^T \tilde{J}_{q_1}(t)\Delta q_1(t)dt,$$

where

$$\tilde{J}_{q_1}(t) = -\tilde{X}(t)\tilde{f}_{q_1}\ , \quad t \in [0,T]$$

holds.

By the matrix differential equation (13) one derives the multipliers λ_i due to the constraints related to the control variables:

$$\dot{\lambda}_i = f_{x_i}\lambda_i + L_{x_i}\ , \quad \lambda_i(T) = 0. \tag{8$'$}$$

The change of the first player's payoff in terms of the original formulation (3) - (7) of the game is given by

$$\Delta J_i = \int_0^T J_{q_1}(t)\Delta q_1(t)dt = \int_0^T (\lambda_1(t)f_{q_1}+L_{q_1})\Delta q_1(t)dt.$$

Hence the first player's changes of the control variable are

$$\Delta q_1 = W_1(t)(L_{q_1}+\lambda_1 f_{q_1})\ , \quad t \in [0,T],$$

where $W_1(t)$ denotes a certain weight function, which has only influence to the rate of convergence of the algorithm.

The constraints of the control variables are considered such that for the changes in each iteration

$$\hat{q}(t) := q(t) + \Delta q(t)$$

one checks, whether they lie inside the admissible control region Q. If not, $\tilde{q}(t) \in Q$ is chosen as a new control function such that the distance between $\hat{q}$ and $\tilde{q}$ becomes minimal, i.e. $\tilde{q}$ is the projection of $\hat{q}$ onto Q.

It is well-known that there are problems related to the convergence of first-order gradient algorithms (see e.g. Bryson and Ho, 1975, or Doležal and Thoma, 1979). The rate of convergence depends on the weights W_i. Hence it may be necessary to perform several trial runs, until suitable convergence forcing weights are found.

The advantage of this first-order gradient algorithm is its independence of the initial choice of control variables. Hence it is not necessary to guess any solutions. In the FORTRAN program, which was written and implemented for this algorithm, the integrations of the differential equations are done by the Runge-Kutta method, and definite integrals are evaluated using Simpson's rule. For the stopping criterium $\varepsilon = 10^{-5}$ is chosen.

Since the numerical solution of differential equations only yields the values of the solution at given points, at each iteration several hundreds of such values have to be computed. Hence the program uses per iteration several minutes total time for computation.

The examples discussed below used 15 - 35 iterations, until convergence. Hence total time for computation amounts to 40 minutes up to a few hours per example. All computations were performed at a Univac 1100/81.

For the determination of suitable weights W_i there exists no theory (see Doležal and Thoma, 1979). Therefore the weights used were found interactively. By trial runs convergence was found out. In case of divergence, new weights were inserted so long, until convergence could be obtained.

Actually this procedure is rather costly yet simple. For more sophisticated algorithms like e.g. the Nash equilibria searching algorithm of L. F. Pau (1975) corresponding results would only be obtained by an even more expensive computation. That could hardly be justified within our budget constraint. Prior to the own model the algorithm was tested with problems, the solutions of which are well-known from the literature (see Joergensen, 1982).

V.2 Specializations of the Basic Model

V.2.1 Fixed Resource Stock

In the sequel we will specialize the above model by assuming several demand and cost functions and present the algorithmic results. One numerical result is that the time horizon T plays an important role for the structure of the solution. If it is chosen relatively small, the solution can be unaffected by the exhaustibility of the resource. For reasons of comparability in all examples the market for an exhaustible resource is partitioned between three oligopolists, one of them possesses an initial amount of the resource twice as big as another one, and the third one lying between these both:
$x_1^0 = 2,\ x_2^0 = 1.7,\ x_3^0 = 1.$
The oligopolist with the biggest resource stock will be called the biggest one or the first one. Both others will be in the respective succession called the second and the third oligopolist. Consequently the latter one will also be called the smallest one.

Example 1:

First recall Example 2 of Chapter IV, where a resource market is introduced with linear demand and linear cost function. The costs were assumed to depend on the total remaining amount of the resource:

$$c_i = c_i(\sum_{i=1}^{N} x_i(t)) = B - b(\sum_{i=1}^{N} x_i(t)). \qquad (1)'$$

I.e. all oligopolists are facing identical extraction costs per unit of the resource at each instant of time, independent on the respective extraction rate.
Each supplier participates at one deposit of the resource and, initially it is fixed, which amount of the deposit belongs to the respective supplier. Now each one can decide, whether he will extract his part of the resource now or later.
There are two decisive aspects:
First the costs are important. They rise even if the oligopolist does not extract at all, provided others do.

Secondly the price, given by supply and demand of the resource, plays a role. However, the price depends, according to the demand function (2), on the total supply of the resource. Consequently the price rises, if one of the suppliers will retard his amount of the resource possibly to zero, and hence the other suppliers can get higher profits.
Moreover, the costs will rise for that oligopolist, who keeps off the market, due to the extraction by the others.
Hence the equilibrium obtained in chapter IV.1 and shown by figure 1 is the only to be met.
Moreover, the algorithm actually produces this solution.

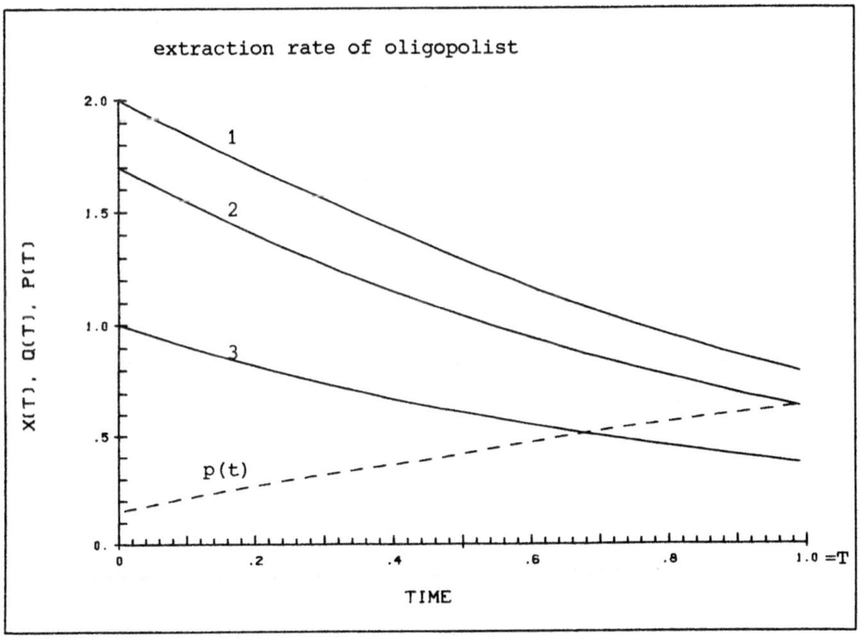

fig. 1

Example 2:

The cost structure of example 1 is generalized into nonidentical costs for all suppliers.
First it is assumed that the costs are the higher, the lower the resource endowment of the oligopolist:

$$c_i = c_i(x_i(t)) = B - bx_i(t) \qquad i=1,2,...,N. \qquad (1)'$$

The constants B and b are assumed to be identical for all suppliers and consequently the smallest oligopolist faces initially the highest costs. (This assumption may be rather arbitrary and will be changed below.)
The effect of this disadvantage to the smaller oligopolists is shown in figure 2.

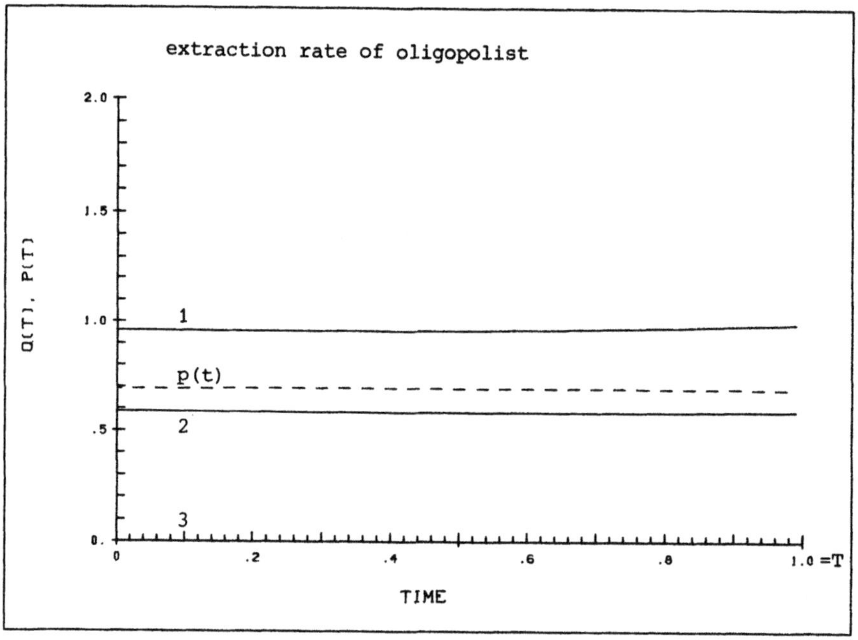

fig. 2

The extraction rate of oligopolist 3 is not shown (see below).

The extraction rates are constant, and the smallest oligopolist does not exploit his reserves at all. Obviously the price of the resource, given by the total supply, cannot compensate the high costs, which he had to expend.
Furthermore, the other ones do not care about the exhaustibility of their amounts of the resource. Otherwise they could not choose constant extraction rates, which necessarily cause the amounts to be totally exhausted at a certain time. This time of ultimate exhaustion can easily be obtained by extrapolating the respective curves (lines) in figure 3.

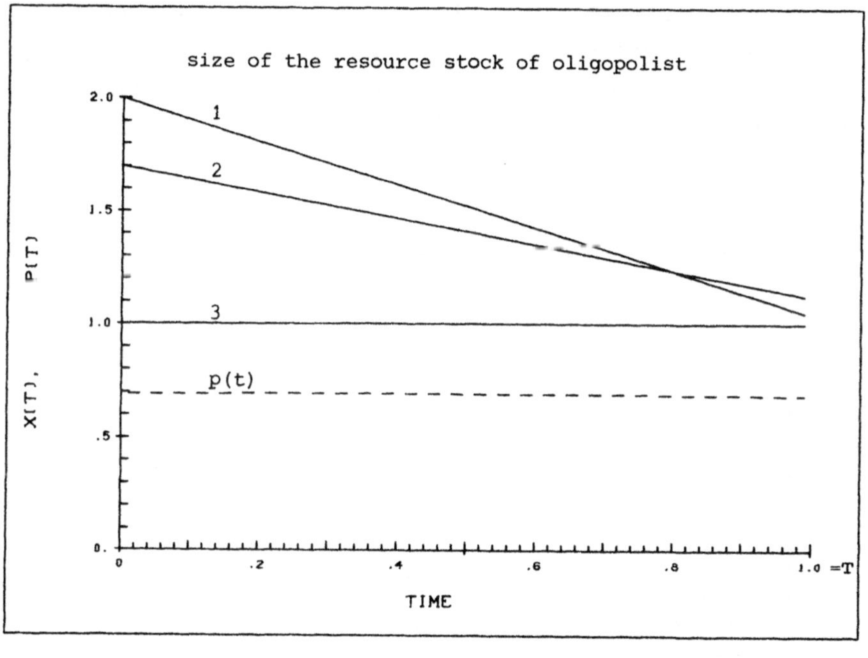

fig. 3

The succession of the exhaustion of the resource stocks is given by the initial endowments of the oligopolists: The biggest one exploits his amount quickest. The reason why can be found in the cost structure and the time horizon T = 1, which is so small that the bigger oligopolists do not need to care about the exhaustibility of their resource stocks.

Moreover, the constant price is high enough throughout the whole period under consideration to compensate for the extraction costs. However, if they would proceed in this manner they would fall into the no supply trap, as already has happened to the smallest one.

Example 3:

In order to find out the sensitivity with respect to ultimate exhaustion a next example is computed. The same cost and demand functions are used, however, the time horizon is enlarged to T = 3. The computational results of the Nash equilibrium are shown in figure 4. Obviously they are different to those ones of example 2.

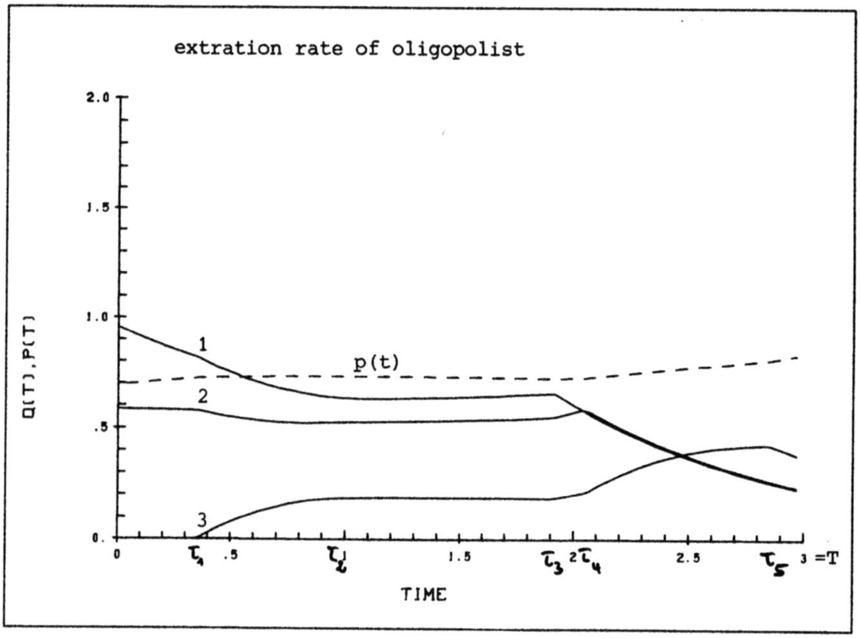

fig. 4

Initially almost the same regime occurs as in example 2: The smallest oligopolist keeps off the market, since the extraction costs are too high. Oligopolist 3 waits supplying, until the market price will have risen up to a level, which is high enough for covering the extraction costs.

From then on, τ_1, the extraction rates of the bigger oligopolists are further decreasing, and simultaneously the extraction rate of the smallest one increases up to a certain level, which is reached at time τ_2. From then on all extraction rates remain constant. This constant level corresponds to all player's initial resource endowments. The difference of this subperiod and the regime of example 2 is the participation of the smallest oligopolist. Prior to τ_2, i.e. during the period $[0,\tau_1]$ the extraction rates of the two bigger ones decreased, now permitting oligopolist 3 to enter the market.

The constant regime ends at time τ_3, when the extraction rate of the first oligopolist, who is actually no longer the biggest one, gets a bend below, while the two other ones increase.

The reason for this policy switch can be seen by figure 5, where the remaining reserves of all oligopolists are plotted:

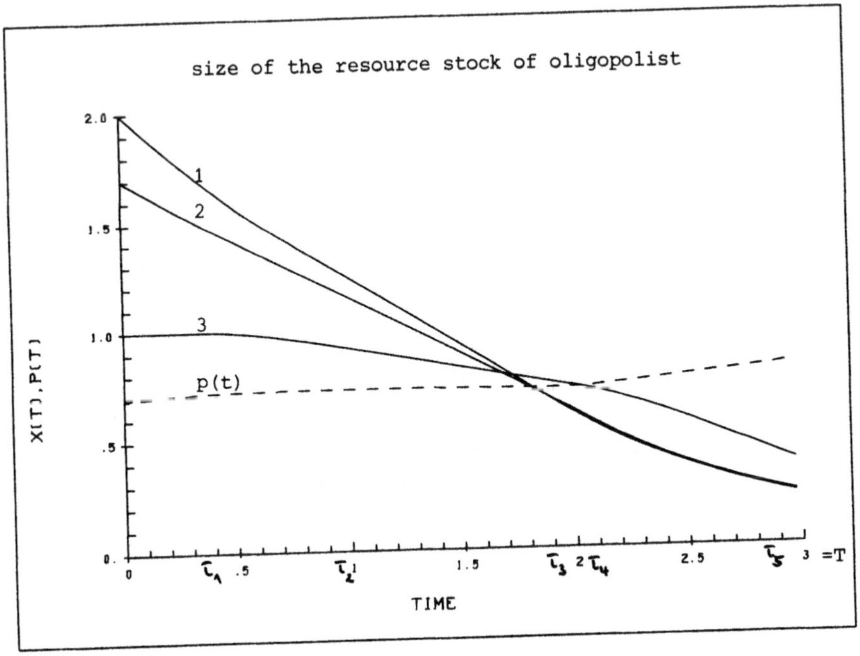

fig. 5

The initially smallest oligopolist is now the biggest one, and the two other ones own reserves of equal size. However, the sizes of these reserves are the only characteristics for the differentiation of the oligopolists. Hence they have to act identically. Therefore the extraction rates of these two "larger" oligopolists converge. This adjustment process ends at time τ_4, when both extraction rates are identical. From now on these two rates decline exponentially and so decrease the respective reserves, too. This regime corresponds to example 1, where the extraction costs of all suppliers were assumed to be identical.

The extraction rate of the third oligopolist, however, increases until time τ_5. During this period his extraction rate exceeds both others, because he is actually the biggest oligopolist, and consequently he extracts most.

From time τ_5 on a stable regime is reached, and all extraction rates decrease exponentially.

The explanation of this regime can be seen in the small differences between all oligopolists. Different extraction costs do no longer cause different extraction policies. I.e. the regime of example 1 is given.

Obviously the oligopolistic market structure equalizes the resource stocks.

Example 4:

In order to prove the stability of this final regime of Example 3 the time horizon is once more postponed, i.e. T = 4. The results are shown by figures 6 and 7.

Obviously the results are principally identical to those of example 3. The main information given by Example 4 can be found in the asymptotic behaviour of the extraction rates and the remaining resource stocks: Since the extraction rates are exponentially decreasing, ultimate exhaustion will be reached only asymptotically.

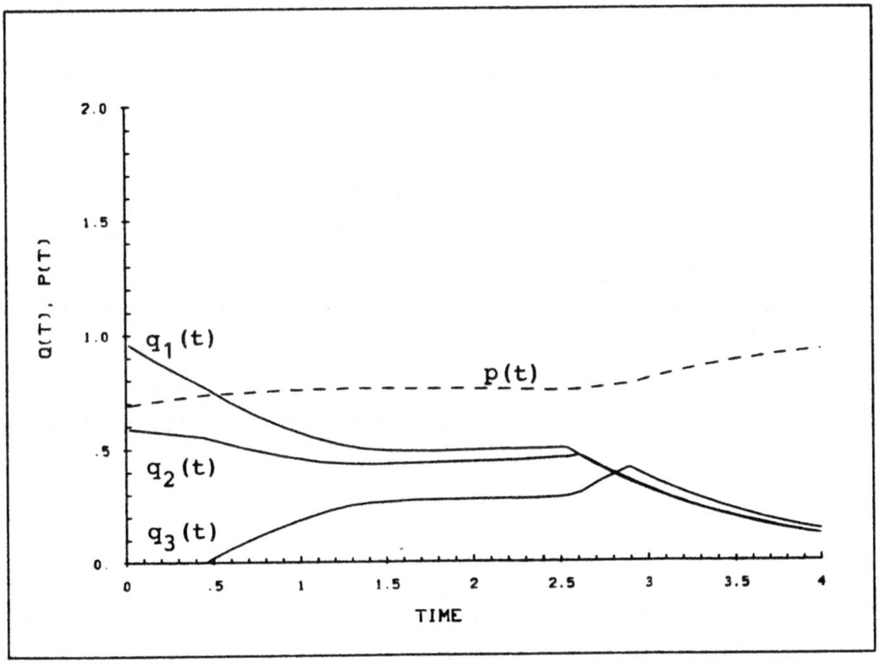
2.0
1.5
1.0
.5
0.
Q(T), P(T)
q_1(t)
p(t)
q_2(t)
q_3(t)
0
.5
1
1.5
2
2.5
3
3.5
4
TIME

fig. 6

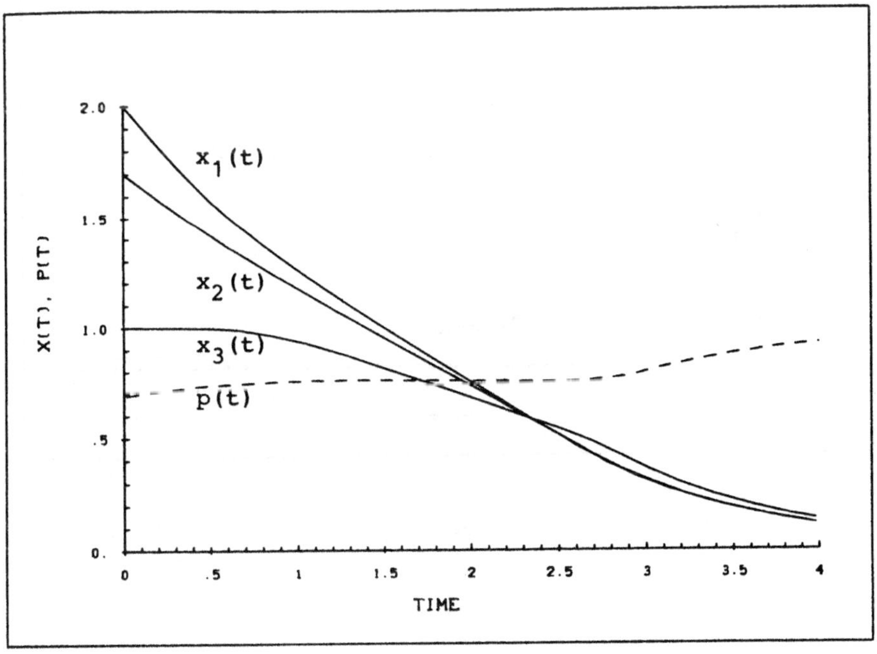
2.0
1.5
1.0
.5
0.
X(T), P(T)
x_1(t)
x_2(t)
x_3(t)
p(t)
0
.5
1
1.5
2
2.5
3
3.5
4
TIME

fig. 7

Example 5:

To show the exponential decline of the extraction rates, the time horizon is once more extended. With the data of examples 3 and 4 an equilibrium is computed for T = 8.

The results are given by figures 8 and 9.

Initially the old regimes are be obtained: The smallest oligopolist, who faces the highest costs, does not extract at all. However, after some time, when the price has risen enough due to the decreasing extraction by the two other oligopolists, he starts depleting, too. From now on the extraction rates of all oligopolists converge, finally becoming identical. I.e. the above adjustment process is obtained.

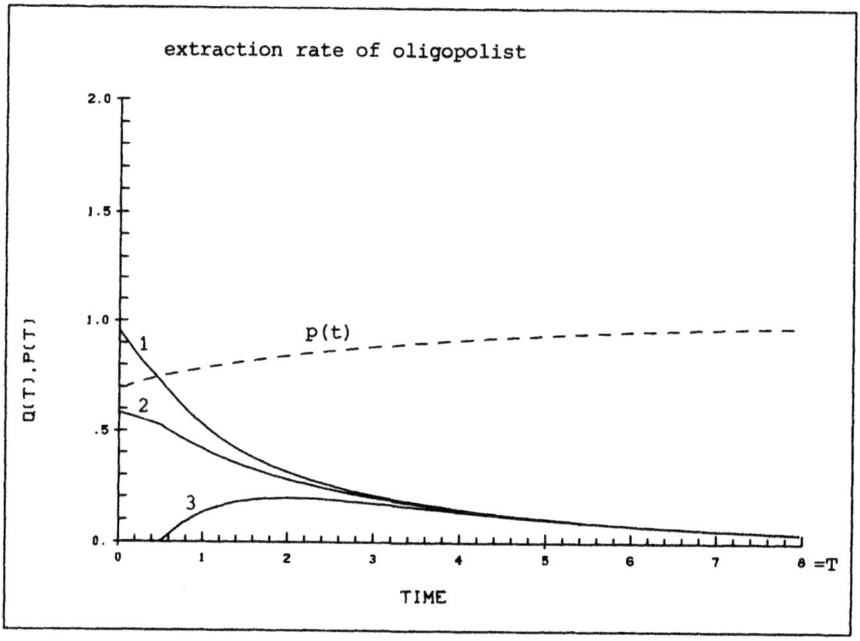

fig. 8

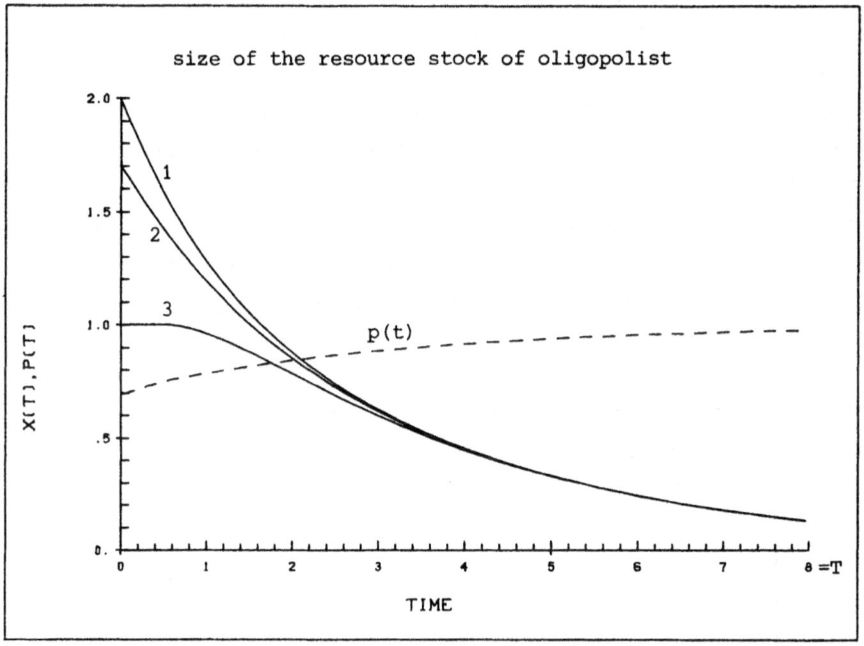

fig. 9

Example 6:

By this example the rather arbitrary assumption of highest costs for the smallest oligopolist is dropped.
Using again the same demand function, however, now assuming the subsequent linear cost functions

$$c_1(x_1(t)) = 1 - 0.15x_1(t) , \quad x_1{}^0 = 2.$$
$$c_2(x_2(t)) = 1 - 0.25x_2(t) , \quad x_2{}^0 = 1.7$$
$$c_3(x_3(t)) = 1 - 0.50x_3(t) , \quad x_3{}^0 = 1.$$

an example of arbitrary linear cost is computed.
Now the smallest oligopolist faces the best and the biggest oligopolist the worst cost structure.
The computed results, plotted in figures 10 and 11, are not very surprising:
Once again a certain adjustment process of the three players can be observed. However, equally sized resource stocks of all oligopolists are not reached. The different cost functions cause the resource

stocks to remain different. Consequently the extraction rates start at levels, which correspond to the levels of the initial costs.
In order to avoid exhaustion, the smallest player's extraction rate decreases fast. Finally the previous regime is given: All extraction rates are strictly monotonocally decreasing, approaching zero asymptotically.
Moreover, it is interesting to note that the price development is obviously independent from the special cost functions of each oligopolist. It is identical with the price of example 5.

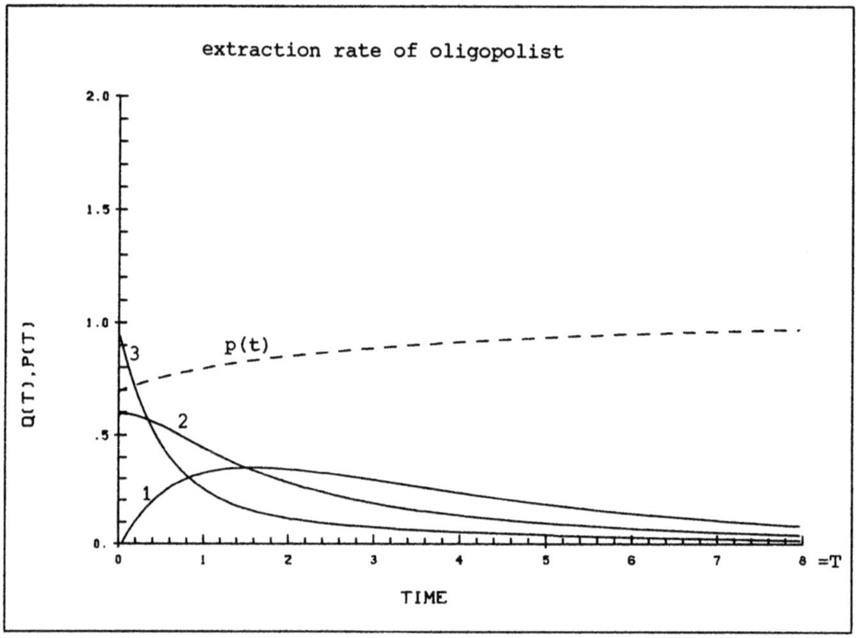

fig. 10

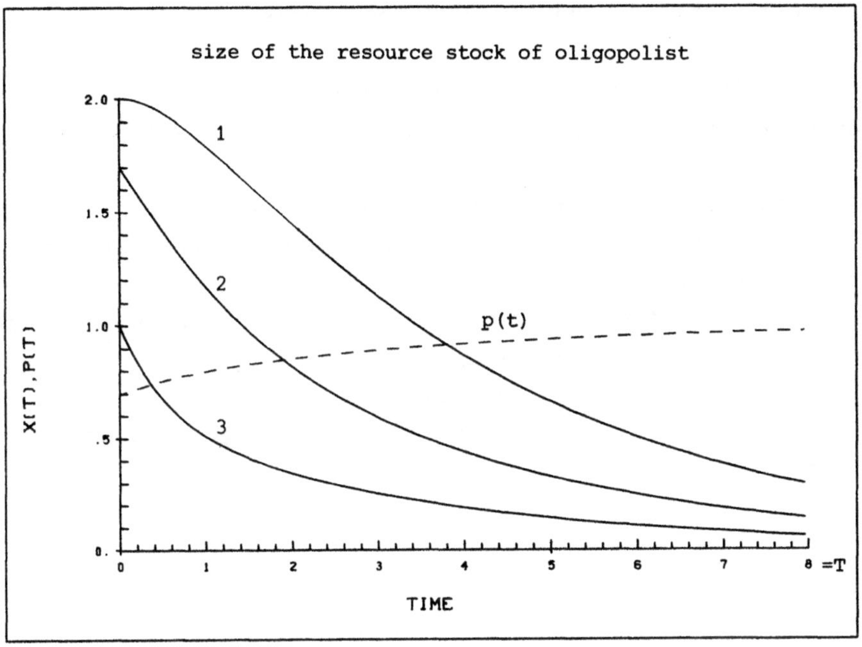
size of the resource stock of oligopolist
2.0
1.5
1.0
.5
0.
X(T),P(T)
1
2
3
p(t)
0
1
2
3
4
5
6
7
8 =T
TIME

fig. 11

V.2.2 Deterministic Expandable Resource Stocks

Different to the preceding section we now assume that the initially available resource stocks can be expanded by exploration of further reserves.
The expansion of the reserves is supposed to be exogenously by postponing extraction of a part of the respective resource stocks. I.e. the increase of the reserves will be proportional to the existing stocks. This assumption makes sense, if it is interpreted as a better technology in depleting the given reserves.
Since we restrict ourselves to obtain the changes of the extraction policy only tendentially, we omit to consider the costs of the new technology.

Example 7:

In order to compare the results with the results of the preceding section we assume the same linear demand and cost functions as above, and consequently the only difference to Example 4 is given by the new state equations

$$\begin{aligned} \dot{x}_i &= -q_i(t) + \alpha x_i(t), \quad 0 < \alpha < 1. \\ x_i(0) &= x_i^0, \quad t \in [0,T]. \end{aligned} \qquad (3)'$$

The results plotted in figures 12 and 13 were computed with $T = 4$ and $\alpha = 0.1$. Obviously they differ from those ones discussed above only slightly (see above pp. 136,137).
Comparing the distances between the remaining resource amounts, one obtains that both initially bigger oligopolists lose versus the third one. Hence the differences of the extraction rates are greater, too. The simplest explanation for this result can be found in the fact that initially the third oligopolist can expand his available resource stock without costs. Hence the proportions switch earlier in comparison with figure 6.
Secondly the possibility of expansion of the available reserves takes only effect on the levels of the extraction rates.

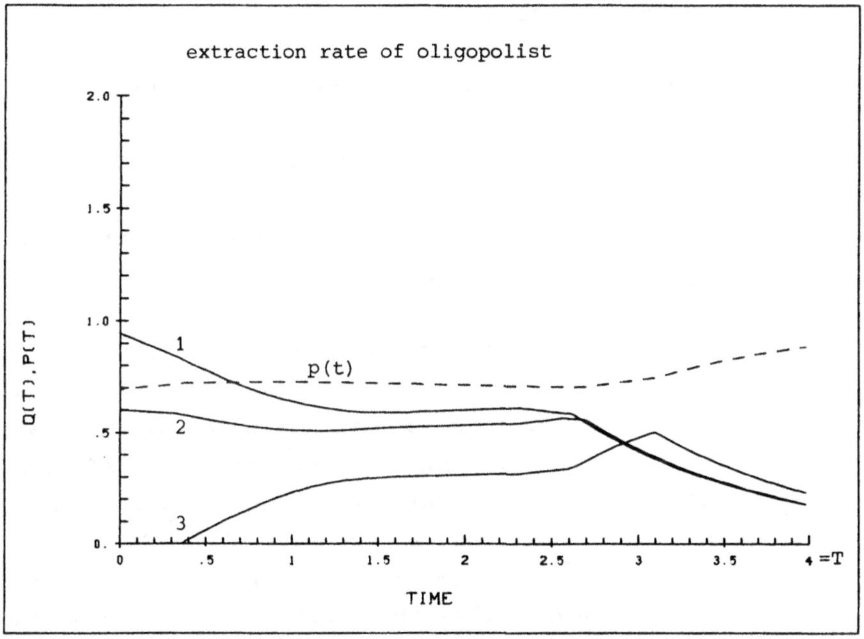
extraction rate of oligopolist
2.0
1.5
1.0
.5
0.
Q(T),P(T)
1
2
3
p(t)
0
.5
1
1.5
2
2.5
3
3.5
4=T
TIME

fig. 12

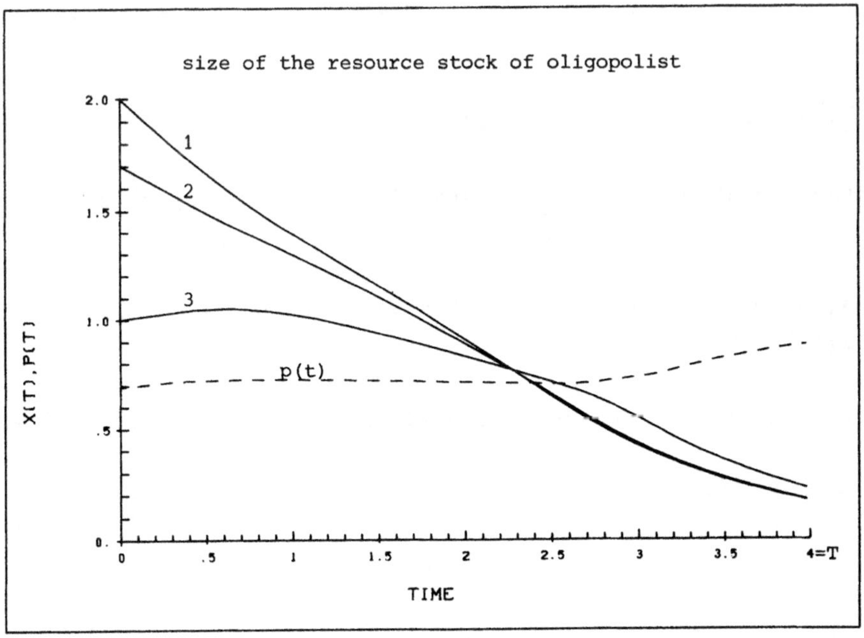
size of the resource stock of oligopolist
2.0
1.5
1.0
.5
0.
X(T),P(T)
1
2
3
p(t)
0
.5
1
1.5
2
2.5
3
3.5
4=T
TIME

fig. 13

V.3 Oligopoly and Price Strategies

Now the assumptions (A2) and (A4) are changed as follows:

(A2)′ Only the prices of the resource can be controlled.

(A4)′ The extraction rates are determined according to the demand given by the respective prices.

Due to the homogeneity of the exhaustible resource all prices must be equal. However, in our case this does not need to be so. Suppose, the extraction capacities of the oligopolists are bounded. Then rationing can happen as follows: The cheapest supplier cannot satisfy the whole demand because of his capacity constraints. The remaining demand will then be satisfied by the next cheaper supplier etc.
Now the cheapest supplier could increase his price so as to adapt it to the other prices. However, then the demand would decrease and this need not be optimal. Hence it is possible that even in a homogeneous oligopoly the prices are different, since oligopolists are of different size and the supplied stocks are finite.
The price-demand relation assumed in the subsequent examples is given by

$$q(t) = e^{-\alpha p(t)}, \quad t \in [0,T], \quad 0 < \alpha < 1. \tag{14}$$

The state equation of the corresponding differential game is then given by

$$\dot{x}_i = -q_i(t) = -e^{-\alpha p_i(t)}, \quad 0 < \alpha < 1, \quad t \in [0,T] \qquad (3)''$$
$$x_i(0) = x_i^0.$$

The initial endowments are once again $x_1^0 = 2$, $x_2^0 = 1.7$, $x_3^0 = 1$.

Example 8:

Here $\alpha = 0.1$ and $T = 1$ are assumed.
The computed results of this example are plotted in figures 14 and 15. Figure 14 shows that the equilibrium prices cause rather low extraction rates.
Moreover, the indirect control of the extraction rates by prices leads to a certain monotonicity in the extraction behaviour of the oligopolists.
They start from clearly different prices, however, with time these prices converge, similarly as quantity behaviour converges.
Further, prices increase exponentially with the rate r, according to Hotelling's rule. Hence the extraction rates decrease, according to (14) and assumption (A5), with the rate α.
The remaining amounts of the resource also decrease with the rate α, according to the state equation (3)" (see figure 15).

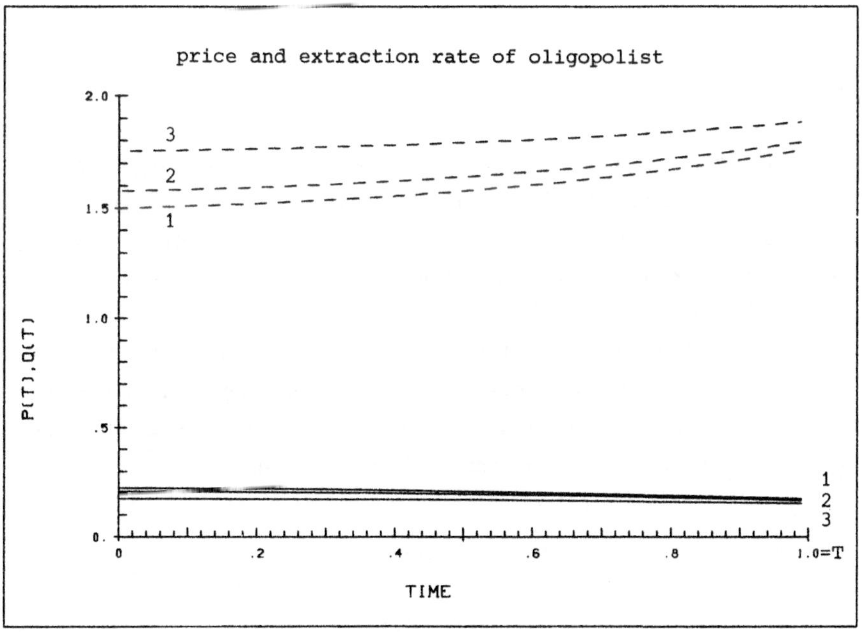

fig. 14

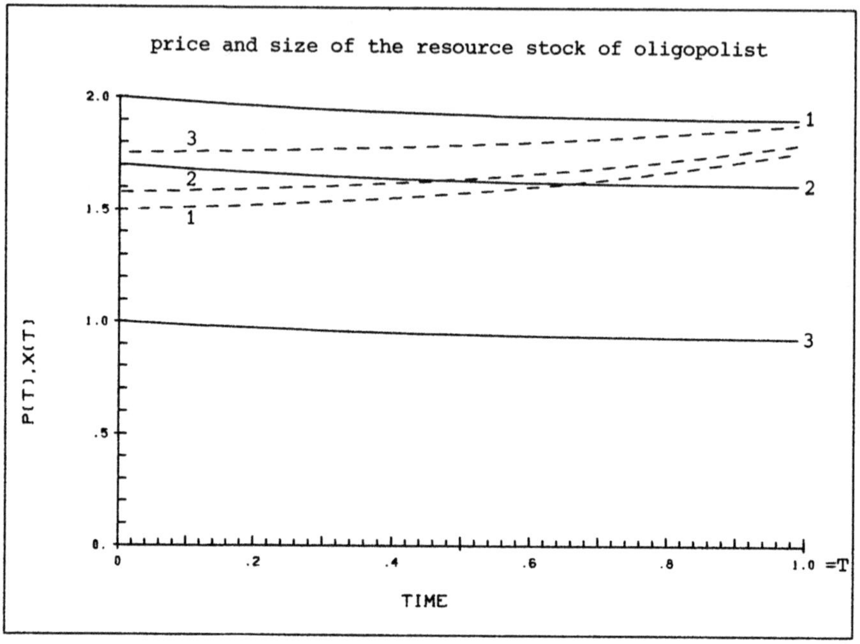

fig. 15

Example 9:

As in section 2 of this chapter the time horizon is extended to T = 3. All other assumptions remain as in Example 8.

The prices start at the same levels as in the preceding example. With time they increase at a rate, compensating the increasing extraction costs (see figure 16).

The main difference between these two examples is given by the slower price convergence. I.e. the changes of the extraction costs are higher due to the greater time horizon and hence the prices of the smaller oligopolists have to increase more than in Example 8.

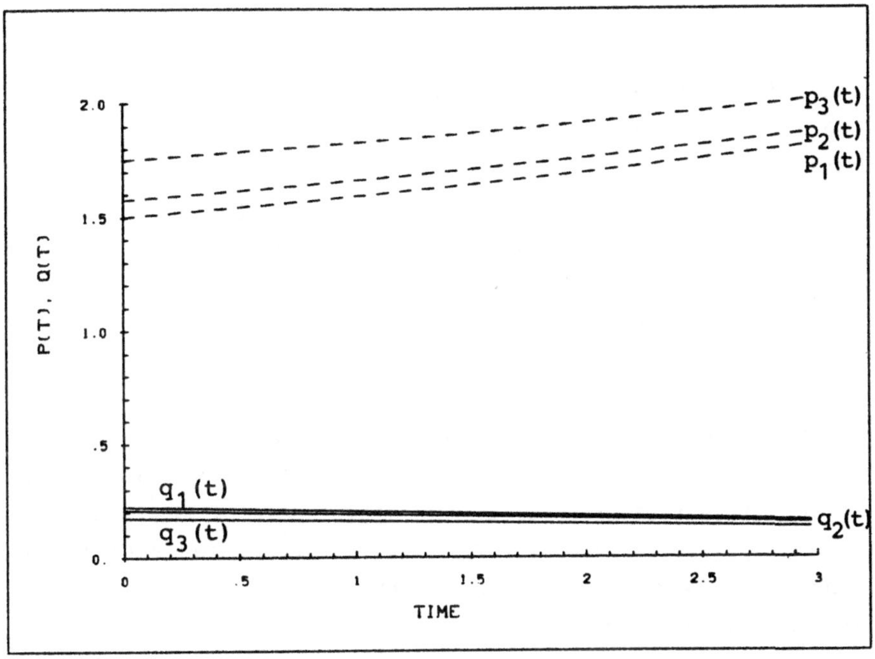
2.0
1.5
1.0
.5
0.
P(T), Q(T)
0
.5
1
1.5
2
2.5
3
TIME
$p_3(t)$
$p_2(t)$
$p_1(t)$
$q_1(t)$
$q_3(t)$
$q_2(t)$

fig. 16

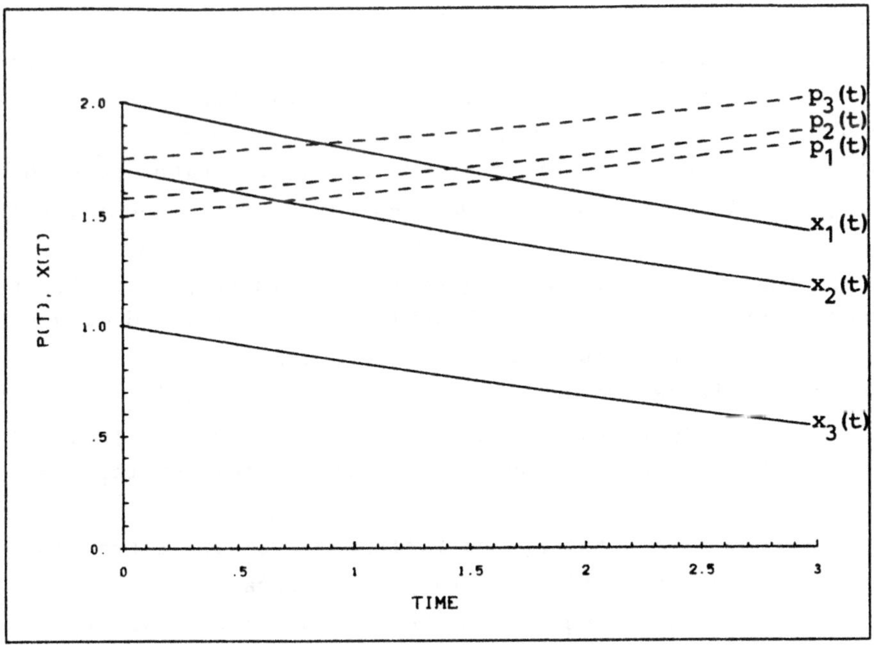
2.0
1.5
1.0
.5
0.
P(T), X(T)
0
.5
1
1.5
2
2.5
3
TIME
$p_3(t)$
$p_2(t)$
$p_1(t)$
$x_1(t)$
$x_2(t)$
$x_3(t)$

fig. 17

V.4 Conclusions

Obviously, from all examples one obtains that the extraction behaviour of the oligopolists do depend sensitively on the cost structure.
The impact of the costs can be seen in comparing example 1 in section V.2 with all other examples of V.2. If the costs are equal for all oligopolists they actually act equally and the level of the extraction rates correspond to the amounts of the resource available to the respective oligopolists.
Secondly one obtains bang-bang controls. I.e. the values of the control functions are at the boundaries of the admissible control regions. At each time the extraction rates are chosen as high as possible and there is no jump to the other side of the boundary of the control region, since the controls are scalar-valued and the state equations are linear with respect to the control variables (see Leitmann, 1981, pp. 212).
Thirdly, provided that the costs per unit of the extracted resource are different, the results differ significantly from the equal cost case. It is even possible that potential suppliers can be held off the market.
Fourthly, the time horizon does matter. If it is chosen sufficiently small, the problem of the exhaustibility of the resource may possibly be of no relevance, provided the resource endowments are high enough. The oligopolists choose their constant extraction rates as high to bar the oligopolist off the market, who has to pay the highest extraction costs.
Obviously this policy cannot be applied indefinitely. Finally the resource reserves are totally exhausted and the excluded oligopolist could supply his reserves at a cost covering rate.
The proof of this regime can be observed by examples 3 - 6 of section V.2. The increasing costs of the supplying oligopolists force down their extraction rates and open the market for the initially excluded competitor.
After a process of adaptation the differences of the extraction costs are equalized and the regime of example 1 occurs.
Summarizing, the market equalizes the oligopolists. However, the planning horizon must be chosen long enough so that the adjustment process can take place.

Finally there is to pay attention to continuity. The algorithm introduced in section V.2. computes continuous controls, though they do not need to be continuous in general. Consequently the adjustment process does not need to be as smooth as described. There may be jumps of the control variables from one level to another one.
The application of price strategies obviously is of minor interest, due to the homogeneity of the resource. But also in this case the policies of the oligopolists converge, i.e. for both kinds of strategies the market equalizes the oligopolists.

BIBLIOGRAPHY

Berkovitz, L.D. (1974). Optimal control theory. Springer-Verlag, New York, Heidelberg, Berlin.

Bryson, A.E., Y.C. Ho (1975). Applied optimal control. Hemisphere Publishing Corporation, Washington, New York, London.

Case J.H. (1969). Toward a theory of many player differential games. SIAM Journal on Control, 7, 179-197.

Case J.H. (1979). Economics and the competitive process. New York University Press, New York.

Chiarella, C. (1980). Optimal depletion of a nonrenewable resource when technical progress is endogenous. In M.C. Kemp, N.V. Long (Hrsg.), Exhaustible resources, optimality, and trade. North-Holland, Amsterdam, 81-94.

Clemhout, S., G. Leitmann, H.Y. Wan (1971). A differential game of duopoly. Econometrica, 39, 911-938.

Cropper, M.L., M.C. Weinstein, R.J. Zeckhauser (1978). The optimal consumption of depletable natural resources: An elaboration, correction, and extension. Quarterly Journal of Economics, 92, 337-344.

Dasgupta, P.S., G. Heal (1974). The optimal depletion of exhaustible resources. Review of Economic Studies, 42, 3-28.

Dasgupta, P.S., G. Heal (1979). Economic theory and exhaustible resources. James Nisbet & Co. Ltd., Cambridge.

Davison, R. (1978). Optimal depletion of an exhaustible resource with research and development towards an alternative technology. Review of Economic Studies, 45, 355-367.

Dirickx, Y.M.I., M. Kok (1982). Resource depletion and R&D programs. In G. Feichtinger (ed.), Optimal control theory and economic analysis. North-Holland, Amsterdam, 269-286.

Dolezal, J., M. Thoma (1979). On the numerical solution of N-player nonzero-sum differential games via Nash solution concept. Problems of Control and Information Theory, 8, 371-385.

Eichhorn, W. (1978). Functional equations in economics. Addison-Wesley, Reading, Mass.

Eichhorn, W., K. Spremann (1982). Efficient pricing of natural resources and intertemporal externalities. In W. Eichhorn, R. Henn, K. Neumann, R. Shephard (eds.), Economic theory of natural resources. Physica-Verlag, Würzburg, 155-174.

Friedman, A. (1971). Differential games. Wiley Interscience, New York.

Funke, H. (1977). Modelle des Mehrproduktenoligopols. Verlag Anton Hain, Meisenheim am Glan.

Gilbert, R.J., S.M. Goldmann (1978). Potential competition and the monopoly price of an exhaustible resource. Journal of Economic Theory, 17, 319-331.

Hadley, G., M.C. Kemp (1971). Variational methods in economics. North-Holland, American Elsevier, New York.

Hanson, D.A. (1979). Increasing extraction costs and resource prices. In R.S. Pindyck (ed.), Advances in the economics of energy and resources, Vol II, JAI Press Inc., Greenwich, Conn., 171-186.

Hoel, M. (1978a). Resource extraction under some alternative market structures. Verlag Anton Hain, Meisenheim am Glan.

Hoel, M. (1978b). Resource extraction, substitute production, and monopoly.Journal of Economic Theory, 19, 28-37.

Hoel, M. (1978c). Resource extraction when a future substitute has an uncertain cost. Review of Economic Studies, 45, 637-644.

Hoel, M. (1980). Extraction of an exhaustible resource under uncertainty. Oelgeschlager, Gunn & Hain, Cambridge, Mass.

Hotelling, H. (1931). The economics of exhaustible resources.Journal of Political Economics, 39, 137-175.

Jorgensen, S. (1982). A survey of some differential games in advertising. Journal of Economic Dynamics and Control, 4, 341-369.

Kamien, M.I., N.L. Schwartz (1978). Optimal exhaustible resource depletion with endogenous technical change. Review of Economic Studies, 45, 179-196.

Kemp, M.C., N.V. Long (1980a). The optimal consumption of depletable resources. In M.C. Kemp, N.V. Long (eds.), Exhaustible resources, optimality, and trade, North-Holland, Amsterdam, 45-54.

Kemp, M.C., N.V. Long (1980b). On the optimal order of exploitation of deposits of an exhaustible resource. In M.C. Kemp, N.V. Long (eds.), Exhaustible resources, optimality, and trade, North-Holland, Amsterdam, 31-40.

Kemp, M.C., N.V. Long (1982). On the development of a substitute for an exhaustible natural resource. In W. Eichhorn, R. Henn, K.Neumann, R. Shephard (eds.), Economic theory of natural resources, Physica-Verlag, Würzburg, 47-64.

Krelle, W. (1976). Preistheorie, 1. Part, J.C.B. Mohr (Paul Siebeck), Tübingen.

Lee, E.B., L. Markus (1967). Foundations of optimal control theory. John Wiley & Sons Inc., New York.

Leitmann, G. (1981). The calculus of variations and optimal control. Plenum Press, New York.

Levhari, D., R.S. Pindyck (1981). The pricing of durable exhaustible resources, Quarterly Journal of Econ., 94, 365-377.

Lévine, J., J. Thepot (1982). Open-loop and closed-loop equilibria in a dynamic duopoly. In G. Feichtinger (eds.), Optimal control theory and economic analysis, North-Holland, Amsterdam, 143-156.

Lewis, T.R., R. Schmalensee (1980). Cartel and oligopoly pricing of nonreplenishable natural resources. In P.T. Liu (eds.), Dynamic optimization and mathematical economics, Plenum Press, New York, 133-156.

Liu, P.T. (1980). Optimum extraction of an exhaustible resource: A Mathematical analysis. In P.T. Liu (eds.), Dynamic optimization and mathematical economics, Plenum Press, New York, 157-168.

Long, N.V. (1977). Optimal exploitation and replenishment of a natural resource. In J.D. Pitchford, S.J. Turnovsky (eds.), Applications of control theory to economic analysis, North-Holland, Amsterdam, 81-106.

Loury, G.C. (1978). The optimal exploitation of an unknown reserve. Review of Economic Studies, 45, 621-636.

Lukes, D.L., D.L. Russel (1971). A global theory for linear-quadratic differential games. Journal of Mathematical Analalysis and Applications, 33, 96-123.

Mehlmann, A. (1982). On relations between open-loop and closed-loop Nash-solutions in deterministic differential games. In G. Feichtinger (eds.), Optimal control theory and economic analysis, North-Holland, Amsterdam, 399-413.

Owen, G. (1971). Spieltheorie. Springer-Verlag, Berlin, Heidelberg, New York.

Pau, L.F. (1975). Differential games and a Nash equilibrium searching algorithm. SIAM Journal on Control, 13, 835-852.

Pau L.F. (1975). Application de la Theorie des Jeux Dynamiques aux Systemes Complexes. Resolution Numerique, Universite de Paris 7, These de Docteur en Sciences.

Peterson, F.M., A.C. Fisher (1977). The exploitation of extractive resources - a survey. Economic Journal, 87, 681-721.

Pindyck, R.S. (1978). The optimal exploration and production of non-renewable resources. Journal of Political Economics, 86, 841-861.

Reinganum, J.F. (1982). A class of differential games for which the closed-loop and open-loop Nash-equilibria coincide. Journal of Optimization Theory and Applications, 36, 253-262.

Salant, S.W. (1976). Exhaustible resources and industrial structure: A Nash-Cournot approach to the world oil market. Journal of Political Economics, 84, 1079-1093.

Salant, S.W. (1982). Imperfect competition in the international energy market: A computerized Nash-Cournot model. Opertions Research, 30, 252-280.

Scalzo, R.C. (1974). N-person linear-quadratic differential games with constraints. SIAM Journal on Control, 12, 419-425.

Siebert, H. (1981). Ökonomische Theorie natürlicher Ressourcen -Ein Überblick. Zeitschrift für Wirtschafts- und Sozialwissenschaften, 101, 267-298.

Simaan, M., J.B.Cruz (1973a). On the Stackelberg strategy in non-zero-sum games. Journal of Optimization Theory and Applications, 11, 533-555.

Simaan, M., J.B.Cruz (1973b). Additional aspects of the Stackelberg strategy in non-zero-sum games. Journal of Optimization Theory and Applications, 11, 613-626.

Simaan, M., T. Takayama (1978). Game theory applied to dynamic duopoly problems with production constraints. Automatica, 14, 161-166.

Solow, R.M. (1974). The Economics of Resources or the Resources of Economics. American Economic Review, 64, 1-14.

Stern, R.J. (1974). Open-loop Nash-equilibrium of N-person nonzero-sum linear-quadratic differential games with magnitude restraints. Journal of Mathematical Analysis and Applications, 46, 352-357.

Starr, A.W., Y.C. Ho (1969a). Nonzero-sum differential games. Journal of Optimization Theory and Applications, 3, 184-206.

Starr, A.W., Y.C. Ho (1969b). Further properties of nonzero-sum differential games. Journal of Optimization Theory and Applications, 3, 207-219.

Stewart, M.B. (1980). Monopoly and the intertemporal production of a durable extractable resource. Quarterly Journal of Economics, 94, 99-111.

Stiglitz, J.E. (1976). Monopoly and the rate of extraction of exhaustible resources. American Economic Review, 66, 655-661.

Ströbele, W., (1984). Wirtschaftswachstum bei begrenzten Energieressourcen. Duncker & Humblot, Berlin.

Sweeney, J.L. (1977). Economics of depletable resources: Market forces and intertemporal bias. Review of Economic Studies, 44, 125-141.

Tolwinski, B. (1979). A method for computing Nash equilibria for non-zero-sum differential games. In J. Stoer (ed.), Optimization techniques, Part 1, Springer-Verlag, Berlin, Heidelberg, New York, 272-281.

Ulph, A.M., G.M. Folie (1980). Exhaustible resources and cartels: An intertemporal Nash-Cournot model. Canadadian Journal of Economics, 13, 645-658.

Varaiya, P. (1970). N-person nonzero-sum differential games with linear dynamics. SIAM Journal on Control, 8, 441-449.

Vidyasagar, M. (1976). A new approach to N-person nonzero-sum linear-quadratic differential games. Journal of Optimization Theory and Applications, 18, 171-175.

Vousden, N. (1973). Basic theoretical issues of resource depletion. Journal of Economic Theory, 6, 126-143.

Vousden, N. (1977a). Resource depletion with possible non-convexities in production. In J.D. Pitchford, S.T. Turnovsky (ed.), Applications of control theory to economic analysis, North-Holland, Amsterdam, 57-80.

Vousden, N. (1977b). Resource scarcity and the availability of substitutes: A theoretical model. In M.D. Intriligator (ed.), Frontiers of quantitative economics, Vol. IIIb, North-Holland, Amsterdam, 507-532.

Weinstein, M.C. R.J. Zeckhauser (1974). Use patterns for depletable and recycleable resources. Review of Economic Studies, 42, 67-88.

Vol. 157: Optimization and Operations Research. Proceedings 1977. Edited by R. Henn, B. Korte, and W. Oettli. VI, 270 pages. 1978.

Vol. 158: L. J. Cherene, Set Valued Dynamical Systems and Economic Flow. VIII, 83 pages. 1978.

Vol. 159: Some Aspects of the Foundations of General Equilibrium Theory: The Posthumous Papers of Peter J. Kalman. Edited by J. Green. VI, 167 pages. 1978.

Vol. 160: Integer Programming and Related Areas. A Classified Bibliography. Edited by D. Hausmann. XIV, 314 pages. 1978.

Vol. 161: M. J. Beckmann, Rank in Organizations. VIII, 164 pages. 1978.

Vol. 162: Recent Developments in Variable Structure Systems, Economics and Biology. Proceedings 1977. Edited by R. R. Mohler and A. Ruberti. VI, 326 pages. 1978.

Vol. 163: G. Fandel, Optimale Entscheidungen in Organisationen. VI, 143 Seiten. 1979.

Vol. 164: C. L. Hwang and A. S. M. Masud, Multiple Objective Decision Making – Methods and Applications. A State-of-the-Art Survey. XII, 351 pages. 1979.

Vol. 165: A. Maravall, Identification in Dynamic Shock-Error Models. VIII, 158 pages. 1979.

Vol. 166: R. Cuninghame-Green, Minimax Algebra. XI, 258 pages. 1979.

Vol. 167: M. Faber, Introduction to Modern Austrian Capital Theory. X, 196 pages. 1979.

Vol. 168: Convex Analysis and Mathematical Economics. Proceedings 1978. Edited by J. Kriens. V, 136 pages. 1979.

Vol. 169: A. Rapoport et al., Coalition Formation by Sophisticated Players. VII, 170 pages. 1979.

Vol. 170: A. E. Roth, Axiomatic Models of Bargaining. V, 121 pages. 1979.

Vol. 171: G. F. Newell, Approximate Behavior of Tandem Queues. XI, 410 pages. 1979.

Vol. 172: K. Neumann and U. Steinhardt, GERT Networks and the Time-Oriented Evaluation of Projects. 268 pages. 1979.

Vol. 173: S. Erlander, Optimal Spatial Interaction and the Gravity Model. VII, 107 pages. 1980.

Vol. 174: Extremal Methods and Systems Analysis. Edited by A. V. Fiacco and K. O. Kortanek. XI, 545 pages. 1980.

Vol. 175: S. K. Srinivasan and R. Subramanian, Probabilistic Analysis of Redundant Systems. VII, 356 pages. 1980.

Vol. 176: R. Färe, Laws of Diminishing Returns. VIII, 97 pages. 1980.

Vol. 177: Multiple Criteria Decision Making-Theory and Application. Proceedings, 1979. Edited by G. Fandel and T. Gal. XVI, 570 pages. 1980.

Vol. 178: M. N. Bhattacharyya, Comparison of Box-Jenkins and Bonn Monetary Model Prediction Performance. VII, 146 pages. 1980.

Vol. 179: Recent Results in Stochastic Programming. Proceedings, 1979. Edited by P. Kall and A. Prékopa. IX, 237 pages. 1980.

Vol. 180: J. F. Brotchie, J. W. Dickey and R. Sharpe, TOPAZ – General Planning Technique and its Applications at the Regional, Urban, and Facility Planning Levels. VII, 356 pages. 1980.

Vol. 181: H. D. Sherali and C. M. Shetty, Optimization with Disjunctive Constraints. VIII, 156 pages. 1980.

Vol. 182: J. Wolters, Stochastic Dynamic Properties of Linear Econometric Models. VIII, 154 pages. 1980.

Vol. 183: K. Schittkowski, Nonlinear Programming Codes. VIII, 242 pages. 1980.

Vol. 184: R. E. Burkard and U. Derigs, Assignment and Matching Problems: Solution Methods with FORTRAN-Programs. VIII, 148 pages. 1980.

Vol. 185: C. C. von Weizsäcker, Barriers to Entry. VI, 220 pages. 1980.

Vol. 186: Ch.-L. Hwang and K. Yoon, Multiple Attribute Decision Making – Methods and Applications. A State-of-the-Art-Survey. XI, 259 pages. 1981.

Vol. 187: W. Hock, K. Schittkowski, Test Examples for Nonlinear Programming Codes. V. 178 pages. 1981.

Vol. 188: D. Bös, Economic Theory of Public Enterprise. VII, 142 pages. 1981.

Vol. 189: A. P. Lüthi, Messung wirtschaftlicher Ungleichheit. IX, 287 pages. 1981.

Vol. 190: J. N. Morse, Organizations: Multiple Agents with Multiple Criteria. Proceedings, 1980. VI, 509 pages. 1981.

Vol. 191: H. R. Sneessens, Theory and Estimation of Macroeconomic Rationing Models. VII, 138 pages. 1981.

Vol. 192: H. J. Bierens: Robust Methods and Asymptotic Theory in Nonlinear Econometrics. IX, 198 pages. 1981.

Vol. 193: J. K. Sengupta, Optimal Decisions under Uncertainty. VII, 156 pages. 1981.

Vol. 194: R. W. Shephard, Cost and Production Functions. XI, 104 pages. 1981.

Vol. 195: H. W. Ursprung, Die elementare Katastrophentheorie. Eine Darstellung aus der Sicht der Ökonomie. VII, 332 pages. 1982.

Vol. 196: M. Nermuth, Information Structures in Economics. VIII, 236 pages. 1982.

Vol. 197: Integer Programming and Related Areas. A Classified Bibliography. 1978 – 1981. Edited by R. von Randow. XIV, 338 pages. 1982.

Vol. 198: P. Zweifel, Ein ökonomisches Modell des Arztverhaltens. XIX, 392 Seiten. 1982.

Vol. 199: Evaluating Mathematical Programming Techniques. Proceedings, 1981. Edited by J.M. Mulvey. XI, 379 pages. 1982.

Vol. 200: The Resource Sector in an Open Economy. Edited by H. Siebert. IX, 161 pages. 1984.

Vol. 201: P. M. C. de Boer, Price Effects in Input-Output-Relations: A Theoretical and Empirical Study for the Netherlands 1949–1967. X, 140 pages. 1982.

Vol. 202: U. Witt, J. Perske, SMS – A Program Package for Simulation and Gaming of Stochastic Market Processes and Learning Behavior. VII, 266 pages. 1982.

Vol. 203: Compilation of Input-Output Tables. Proceedings, 1981. Edited by J. V. Skolka. VII, 307 pages. 1982.

Vol. 204: K.C. Mosler, Entscheidungsregeln bei Risiko: Multivariate stochastische Dominanz. VII, 172 Seiten. 1982.

Vol. 205: R. Ramanathan, Introduction to the Theory of Economic Growth. IX, 347 pages. 1982.

Vol. 206: M.H. Karwan, V. Lotfi, J. Telgen, and S. Zionts, Redundancy in Mathematical Programming. VII, 286 pages. 1983.

Vol. 207: Y. Fujimori, Modern Analysis of Value Theory. X, 165 pages. 1982.

Vol. 208: Econometric Decision Models. Proceedings, 1981. Edited by J. Gruber. VI, 364 pages. 1983.

Vol. 209: Essays and Surveys on Multiple Criteria Decision Making. Proceedings, 1982. Edited by P. Hansen. VII, 441 pages. 1983.

Vol. 210: Technology, Organization and Economic Structure. Edited by R. Sato and M.J. Beckmann. VIII, 195 pages. 1983.

Vol. 211: P. van den Heuvel, The Stability of a Macroeconomic System with Quantity Constraints. VII, 169 pages. 1983.

Vol. 212: R. Sato and T. Nôno, Invariance Principles and the Structure of Technology. V, 94 pages. 1983.

Vol. 213: Aspiration Levels in Bargaining and Economic Decision Making. Proceedings, 1982. Edited by R. Tietz. VIII, 406 pages. 1983.

Vol. 214: M. Faber, H. Niemes und G. Stephan, Entropie, Umweltschutz und Rohstoffverbrauch. IX, 181 Seiten. 1983.

Vol. 215: Semi-Infinite Programming and Applications. Proceedings, 1981. Edited by A.V. Fiacco and K.O. Kortanek. XI, 322 pages. 1983.

Vol. 216: H.H. Müller, Fiscal Policies in a General Equilibrium Model with Persistent Unemployment. VI, 92 pages. 1983.

Vol. 217: Ch. Grootaert, The Relation Between Final Demand and Income Distribution. XIV, 105 pages. 1983.

Vol. 218: P. van Loon, A Dynamic Theory of the Firm: Production, Finance and Investment. VII, 191 pages. 1983.

Vol. 219: E. van Damme, Refinements of the Nash Equilibrium Concept. VI, 151 pages. 1983.

Vol. 220: M. Aoki, Notes on Economic Time Series Analysis: System Theoretic Perspectives. IX, 249 pages. 1983.

Vol. 221: S. Nakamura, An Inter-Industry Translog Model of Prices and Technical Change for the West German Economy. XIV, 290 pages. 1984.

Vol. 222: P. Meier, Energy Systems Analysis for Developing Countries. VI, 344 pages. 1984.

Vol. 223: W. Trockel, Market Demand. VIII, 205 pages. 1984.

Vol. 224: M. Kiy, Ein disaggregiertes Prognosesystem für die Bundesrepublik Deutschland. XVIII, 276 Seiten. 1984.

Vol. 225: T.R. von Ungern-Sternberg, Zur Analyse von Märkten mit unvollständiger Nachfragerinformation. IX, 125 Seiten. 1984

Vol. 226: Selected Topics in Operations Research and Mathematical Economics. Proceedings, 1983. Edited by G. Hammer and D. Pallaschke. IX, 478 pages. 1984.

Vol. 227: Risk and Capital. Proceedings, 1983. Edited by G. Bamberg and K. Spremann. VII, 306 pages. 1984.

Vol. 228: Nonlinear Models of Fluctuating Growth. Proceedings, 1983. Edited by R.M. Goodwin, M. Krüger and A. Vercelli. XVII, 277 pages. 1984.

Vol. 229: Interactive Decision Analysis. Proceedings, 1983. Edited by M. Grauer and A.P. Wierzbicki. VIII, 269 pages. 1984.

Vol. 230: Macro-Economic Planning with Conflicting Goals. Proceedings, 1982. Edited by M. Despontin, P. Nijkamp and J. Spronk. VI, 297 pages. 1984.

Vol. 231: G.F. Newell, The M/M/∞ Service System with Ranked Servers in Heavy Traffic. XI, 126 pages. 1984.

Vol. 232: L. Bauwens, Bayesian Full Information Analysis of Simultaneous Equation Models Using Integration by Monte Carlo. VI, 114 pages. 1984.

Vol. 233: G. Wagenhals, The World Copper Market. XI, 190 pages. 1984.

Vol. 234: B.C. Eaves, A Course in Triangulations for Solving Equations with Deformations. III, 302 pages. 1984.

Vol. 235: Stochastic Models in Reliability Theory. Proceedings, 1984. Edited by S. Osaki and Y. Hatoyama. VII, 212 pages. 1984.

Vol. 236: G. Gandolfo, P.C. Padoan, A Disequilibrium Model of Real and Financial Accumulation in an Open Economy. VI, 172 pages. 1984.

Vol. 237: Misspecification Analysis. Proceedings, 1983. Edited by T.K. Dijkstra. V, 129 pages. 1984.

Vol. 238: W. Domschke, A. Drexl, Location and Layout Planning. IV, 134 pages. 1985.

Vol. 239: Microeconomic Models of Housing Markets. Edited by K. Stahl. VII, 197 pages. 1985.

Vol. 240: Contributions to Operations Research. Proceedings, 1984. Edited by K. Neumann and D. Pallaschke. V, 190 pages. 1985.

Vol. 241: U. Wittmann, Das Konzept rationaler Preiserwartungen. XI, 310 Seiten. 1985.

Vol. 242: Decision Making with Multiple Objectives. Proceedings, 1984. Edited by Y.Y. Haimes and V. Chankong. XI, 571 pages. 1985.

Vol. 243: Integer Programming and Related Areas. A Classified Bibliography 1981–1984. Edited by R. von Randow. XX, 386 pages. 1985.

Vol. 244: Advances in Equilibrium Theory. Proceedings, 1984. Edited by C.D. Aliprantis, O. Burkinshaw and N.J. Rothman. II, 235 pages. 1985.

Vol. 245: J.E.M. Wilhelm, Arbitrage Theory. VII, 114 pages. 1985.

Vol. 246: P.W. Otter, Dynamic Feature Space Modelling, Filtering and Self-Tuning Control of Stochastic Systems. XIV, 177 pages. 1985.

Vol. 247: Optimization and Discrete Choice in Urban Systems. Proceedings, 1983. Edited by B.G. Hutchinson, P. Nijkamp and M. Batty. VI, 371 pages. 1985.

Vol. 248: Plural Rationality and Interactive Decision Processes. Proceedings, 1984. Edited by M. Grauer, M. Thompson and A.P. Wierzbicki. VI, 354 pages. 1985.

Vol. 249: Spatial Price Equilibrium: Advances in Theory, Computation and Application. Proceedings, 1984. Edited by P. T. Harker. VII, 277 pages. 1985.

Vol. 250: M. Roubens, Ph. Vincke, Preference Modelling. VIII, 94 pages. 1985.

Vol. 251: Input-Output Modeling. Proceedings, 1984. Edited by A. Smyshlyaev. VI, 261 pages. 1985.

Vol. 252: A. Birolini, On the Use of Stochastic Processes in Modeling Reliability Problems. VI, 105 pages. 1985.

Vol. 253: C. Withagen, Economic Theory and International Trade in Natural Exhaustible Resources. VI, 172 pages. 1985.

Vol. 254: S. Müller, Arbitrage Pricing of Contingent Claims. VIII, 151 pages. 1985.

Vol. 255: Nondifferentiable Optimization: Motivations and Applications. Proceedings, 1984. Edited by V.F. Demyanov and D. Pallaschke. VI, 350 pages. 1985.

Vol. 256: Convexity and Duality in Optimization. Proceedings, 1984. Edited by J. Ponstein. V, 142 pages. 1985.

Vol. 257: Dynamics of Macrosystems. Proceedings, 1984. Edited by J.-P. Aubin, D. Saari and K. Sigmund. VI, 280 pages. 1985.

Vol. 258: H. Funke, Eine allgemeine Theorie der Polypol- und Oligopolpreisbildung. III, 237 pages. 1985.

Vol. 259: Infinite Programming. Proceedings, 1984. Edited by E.J. Anderson and A.B. Philpott. XIV, 244 pages. 1985.

Vol. 260: H.-J. Kruse, Degeneracy Graphs and the Neighbourhood Problem. VIII, 128 pages. 1986.

Vol. 261: Th.R. Gulledge, Jr., N.K. Womer, The Economics of Made-to-Order Production. VI, 134 pages. 1986.

Vol. 262: H.U. Buhl, A Neo-Classical Theory of Distribution and Wealth. V, 146 pages. 1986.

Vol. 263: M. Schäfer, Resource Extraction and Market Structure. XI, 154 pages. 1986.

GPSR Compliance

The European Union's (EU) General Product Safety Regulation (GPSR) is a set of rules that requires consumer products to be safe and our obligations to ensure this.

If you have any concerns about our products, you can contact us on ProductSafety@springernature.com

In case Publisher is established outside the EU, the EU authorized representative is:

Springer Nature Customer Service Center GmbH
Europaplatz 3
69115 Heidelberg, Germany

Batch number: 10844827

Printed by Printforce, the Netherlands